DRUGS FOR THE MIND

DRUGS FOR THE MIND / SOFIE SUN

CENSORSHIP IN CHINA

Translation
Cômeng Tang

EVATASFOUNDATION

Amsterdam 2015

/ TABLE
OF CONTENTS

/ PREFACE

In the summer of 2011, I had my first encounter with the Chinese censorship system. Before that moment, my knowledge of censorship was mostly limited to hearsay. I remember not being able to refrain from thinking that the things I have heard were but exaggerations of reality, the "complaints"—if not the outright fabrications—of dissidents and disgruntled authors who were out to destroy the reputation of the Communist Party of China. My naive view of censorship in China was thoroughly shattered in the summer of 2011.

At the time, I was accompanying the Dutch poet Ramsy Nasr to visit the Chinese artist Ai Weiwei. Our destination was Caochangdi, Chaoyang District—the workshop of Ai Weiwei in Beijing. When we arrived at his doorsteps, the CCTV cameras above the entrance were the first thing that caught my eye. When I turned my head, I noticed the police officer in a Shanghai Volkswagen automobile who was monitoring the workshop. When I returned my attention to the workshop, I finally noticed that there was a plainclothes officer across the street. That experience made me suddenly realised the grim nature of Chinese censorship and its real life consequences.

You might know Ai Weiwei, the artist and political activist, from his frequent appearance in western media. However, many Chinese would not know of the person Ai Weiwei. Whenever I raise his name in front of my friends and classmates in China, I only elicit a blank expression and receive the following response: "Who is Ai Weiwei?"

I should note that these are urbanites of my same age and who have gone to the same university. Nevertheless, the Chinese state has still managed to mask the existence of one single dissident in spite of the ever growing ubiquity of the Internet in China. This is an astonishing feat—if we were to actually praise censorship.

Of course, censorship could be part of a bigger problem. For instance, my friends might simply have no interest in following the affairs of Ai Weiwei. It is also a fact that my generation lack political awareness—I also did not have any interest in Chinese politics before I left China in 2007. I was an unquestioning student who only thought of studying. Politics did not matter to me if it did not improve my chances of being accepted into a good university. Nevertheless, news broadcasts would usually either report on state visits from various country heads or focus on the party leaders when they are surveying poor regions in China. However, what would come out of these inspections then? Even after surveying for one year, it is more than likely that poverty would still be endemic to those regions.

Censorship would prevent such negative news from reaching the ears of the public. The only exception would be reports on the punishment of dissidents and extremists.

Although these announcements served as warnings to the Chinese public, human rights watchdogs would usually bring such news to international attention in order to pressure the Chinese government into releasing political prisoners. This tactic might have been successful in one or two cases in the past, but the state has decided to stop with these public announcements since the early 2000s.

Shortly after my experience in Beijing, I had the opportunity to meet Mian Mian—an independent writer from China—and learnt of the hardships in her writing career. Two years later in Amsterdam, I met with Ye Fu, another independent writer. His history and his experiences after the Tiananmen-incident had left me stunned and speechless. These encounters with Ye Fu, Mian Mian and Ai Weiwei had finally caused me to wonder the following about China:

"Using cruel methods and pushing people to the brink of desolation just to prevent them from freely expressing themselves; what is wrong with this country?

In 2013, the "Eva Tas Foundation" invited me to write this book on the subject of the Chinese censorship system. You could probably fill a whole bookstore with books dedicated to the topic of censorship. In order to make this a more manageable project— and for the sake of brevity—I had decided to limit my enquiry to literary publications. Literature can be both fiction as well as non-fiction. Its stories can draw readers into a fictional world and at the same time be a discourse on history and reveal its secrets. I was driven by the question of how censorship would operate in the literary world

Facts show that Chinese censors can be enormously cruel in the literary world. Although China has entered the 21st century, Chinese authors—and their loved ones—can still risk publication bans, house arrests, imprisonment, just for criticising the Communist Party of China. I could not believe these facts, nor could I even imagine the severity of the problem until I started interviewing the victims myself. I found myself being left astonished on numerous occasions during my investigation; and many times, I would think that this cannot continue in this manner. Many victims of the regime have remained silent out of fear for further persecution; nevertheless, there are still people who are brave enough to resist even when they are battered and bruised. They are driven by the conviction that the truth will be known by the whole world someday. They will continue to perform their duties as an author until that day comes.

/ INTRODUCTION

In 1957, Lao She, one of China's most influential intellectuals, published an article called "Freedom and Authors" in the magazine *People's China*—an English periodical in China. In the article Lao She proposed the following in the article:

"Authors should write about the things they find interesting and are knowledgeable on. Whether it is the subject matter, the people, their lives or the themes in their work, authors should have complete freedom in what they want to write. If something is worth writing about—and it does not lead people astray—then it should be allowed to be published. Allowing authors to compose and to publish is akin to letting hundred flowers bloom."[1]

These words reflected the kind of world Lao She wanted to live in. However, there is often a marked difference between the ideals of people and their actual situation.

This book focuses on the question whether there is freedom of expression in Chinese literature. I try to answer this question through eleven vignettes; each vignette is focused on the writing career of an independent author (Chapter 1), an exiled author (Chapter 2) or a state-employed author (Chapter 3). I focus primarily on authors of book publications.

Unfortunately, I could not include a discussion of magazine publications or online authors due to space constraints.

I explore how censorship has shaped the historical development and literary landscape of contemporary China. Because not everyone has some affinity with the development of contemporary Chinese literature or the history of modern Chinese history, I will first introduce a few basic historical concepts related to the development of the People's Republic of China. After that, I will talk about a few principles of the Chinese censorship system.

Tushou Chen, *Do the Heavens Know that the People are Sick? A record of the literary world of China after 1949* (Chinese) (Beijing: People's Literature Publishing House, 2013), 106.

_ A QUICK LESSON ON CHINESE HISTORY

Chinese literature is not only an art form similar to western literature, but it also performs a social role in society and politics. However, the political value of Chinese literature has often out-weighted its aesthetic appeal in the history of modern China. In 1930, a group of left-wing authors established the "Author's Alliance" in China. The alliance created a manifesto, inspired by Soviet principles that delineated the social role of authors and literature in society.[2] One of the key points during one of their general assembly specifically stated:

"Art is for social development—it is an instrument for liberating the people. Capitalism hinders the development path of an individual; therefore, the proletariat can only liberate itself through class-struggle. Literary works should in effect reflect the spirit of anti-feudalism, anti-capitalism and anti-bourgeoisie."

Apart from these provisions, the general assembly also set goals for bringing literature closer to the people. As the Chinese population consisted mostly of working and rural class people at the time, the alliance decreed that the language of literary works should be simple enough to allow all people to understand it, even if they have received next to no education.[3]

In 1942, Mao Zedong based his speech on the aforementioned manifesto during the "Yan'an Forum on Literature and Art." He also stressed the social value of literature and arts; however, he stressed that it needs to be used as propaganda tool for the communist revolution and the Communist Party of China. Mao Zedong was of the opinion that art and literature are created to serve the people. However, Mao Zedong strictly understood farmers, labourers and the military as the "people" because ninety percent of the Chinese population was composed of these three social groups. Authors and artists had to study Marxism and experience the life of the common folk in order to "enrich" their knowledge about society. Those who did not follow these social guidelines would suffer the consequences: some of them would be sent to a rural village for hard labour, others were sent to prison, while some authors have even been tortured to the point of committing suicide.[4]

---

2 Douwe Wessel Fokkema, *Report from Peking: Observations of a Western Diplomat on the Cultural Revolution* (London: C. Hurst, 1971), 55.; R. Keith Schoppa, *The Columbia Guide to Modern Chinese History* (New York: Columbia University Press, 2000), 169.

3 Fokkema, *Report from Peking*, 55-56.

4 Schoppa, *The Columbia Guide to Modern Chinese History*, 97-98; 290-291.; Wilt Idema and Lloyd Haft, *Chinese letterkunde: een inleiding* (Dutch) (Amsterdam: Amsterdam University Press, 2005), 278.

Wang Shiwei is one among many who had died due to political persecution. Before the establishment of the People's Republic of China, Wang Shiwei wrote an essay in 1942 called "Politicians and Artists" where he stressed the equal importance of politicians and artists in society. Wang Shiwei's argument was a radical idea for its time. He argued that the communist leaders were susceptible to "being contaminated by the vices of old China" and they would eventually turn into the oppressors that they were waging a revolutionary war on. These words were equal to heresy at the time, as the Chinese people regarded the communist party as their saviours. A critique on their beneficial leaders would be the same as an attack on the people.

The intellectual stance proposed by Wang Shiwei belongs to the May Fourth Movement—essentially a protest movement in the early 20th century that opposed imperialism and the old feudal societal values of China. This rebellious ideology was inherently incompatible with Mao Zedong's ideology, and subsequently, led to the "Yan'an Rectification Campaign"—the first ideological mass movement in the People's Republic of China that was aimed at repressing such non-communist ideologies. Wang Shiwei, as a party member, had to change his stance or he would face the consequences. However, Wang was uncompromising in his political sensibilities and he became an enemy to the party and the revolution.

Wang Shiwei suffered one tragedy after another. The party leadership would constantly harass him with interrogations and struggle sessions, and ordered him to write self-criticisms. The party finally expelled Wang Shiwei and arrested him on April first, 1943, because Wang Shiwei remained critical of the party. Mao Zedong stated that he could not let Wang Shiwei roam freely, but promised to spare him from the death sentence. However, Mao went back on his promise and Wang Shiwei was trialled and sentenced to death in 1947.[5]

After the establishment of the People's Republic of China, a new literary institution was born—the Chinese Writers' Association. Many authors who became a member of the association received a monthly stipend from the state. In their daily "labour," each member had to follow the directions and guidelines of the Communist Party of China. Furthermore, the party also nationalised news, publications and book sales. Authors were "re-educated" in Marxist literature. This meant that the party mandated authors to participate in all kinds of labour and activities that did not necessarily relate to the literary profession. Party ideology dictated that it was necessary for authors to do this kind of work in order to better understand the people. Authors

5 Timothy Cheek, "The Fading of Wild Lilies: Wang Shiwei and Mao Zedong's Yan'an Talks in the First CPC Rectification Movement," *The Australian Journal of Chinese Affairs*, no. 11 (1984): 25–58.
6 Idema and Haft, *Chinese letterkunde*, 280-281.

would often be ploughing the fields or doing construction work.[6]

In an attempt to preserve the purity of the party, a series of anti-corruption and anti-waste campaigns were held from the 1950s until the early 1960s. Some of these campaigns were the "Three Anti" campaign of 1951-52 (against corruption, waste and bureaucracy) and the "Five Anti" campaign of 1952 (bribery, embezzlement, tax evasion, cheating on government contracts, stealing state economic information). The former campaign mainly targeted party cadres, whereas the latter campaign was aimed at wiping out the remnants of what is thought to be bourgeois resistance in Chinese society. From 1952, the *People Daily* would publish self-criticisms of professors, scholars, experts and other professionals. The party targeted these people because it considered their professions and educations to stem from western bourgeois ideology. As the communist ideal is diametrically opposed to bourgeois thought, the party attempted to eradicate these last vestiges of the bourgeoisie.[7]

The communist party felt it was becoming complacent in spite of its many accomplishments. The party leadership encouraged the population to actively criticise the party in an effort to further improve their policies and to gauge the public opinion. Mao Zedong initially thought that the criticisms would not be too severe; however, the results went against his expectations. During 1956, in what came to be known as the "Hundred Flowers Campaign," intellectuals could freely express their long repressed criticisms of the communist party. This promptly led to the "Anti-Rightists Campaign" in 1957 in order to rectify the situation. The state arrested and punished the people—and their families—who held a critical opinion of the party, the so-called "rightists."[8] After this incident, Chinese intellectuals slowly lost the courage to speak their mind.

Starting from the 1930s, the political tone in Chinese literature had started to become increasingly stronger. Under the political leadership of Mao Zedong, authors received the modest job title of "Cultural Labourers." They were unable to choose their own subject matter in their works; everything had to be in the interest of the revolution and the communist party. The resulting work mass produced nearly identical literature, devoid of any human character. Literature that was supposed to be "political" or "communist" works seemed as if they were written by one single entity.[9] Lao She—the intellectual from the beginning of this historical overview—had already foreseen the consequences of such a situation:

7 Tushou Chen, *Life Situations of Chinese Professors in 1950s and 1960s* (Chinese) (Beijing: SDX Joint Publishing Company, 2013), 2-3.

8 Schoppa, *The Columbia Guide to Modern Chinese History*, 155; 158.

9 Mark Leenhouts, *Chinese literatuur van nu: aards maar bevlogen* (Dutch) (Breda: De Geus, 2008), 45.

"We should not prevent authors to develop their own style, but we should encourage it instead. Literary works come in many shapes and colours; they are not identical to each other. If something different comes along, we should not be averse to it, but embrace the difference and encourage it to develop."[10]

In the period of 1962-1965, all facets of Chinese society had already become extremely politicised. If you wanted to be an author, you would only be able to write two kinds of literary works:

1 works that praise and laud the communist party;
2 works that are about the class struggle between the proletariat and the bourgeoisie.

In both cases, it is assumed that you will thoroughly vilify western capitalism.

In 1965, Yao Wenyuan—literary critic, and later blamed for the Cultural Revolution as one of the "Gang of Four"—criticised the opera "Hai Rui Dismissed from Office" written by Wu Han, the then vice-mayor of Beijing. Yao Wenyuan wrote in an article that the play refers to the incident of the dismissal of minister of Defence Peng Dehuai at the "Lushan Conference" in 1959. During this conference, Peng Dehuai was critical of the "Great Leap Forward." Mao Zedong promptly dismissed Peng Dehuai from his position, as he felt that the criticism was targeted in his direction. Yao Wenyuan accused the opera play of being anti-party and anti-socialist, but he probably could not have foreseen that this very article would turn out to be the impetus that would start the "Cultural Revolution."[11]

From 1966 until the late 1970s, Chinese literature would undergo a political "baptism." During the Cultural Revolution, the Red Guards fully enacted Mao Zedong's slogan to "Destroy the Four Olds" (Old Customs, Old Culture, Old Habits, and Old Ideas). Traditional thought, customs, values and culture were all subject to the Red Guards' mission. Temples, museums, libraries and their archives, the writings of domestic and western intellectuals, all would meet destruction during the Cultural Revolution. After destroying the old, the Red Guards would turn their violence to people associated with the Four Olds, namely the former bourgeoisie, intellectuals and cultural elites. Anti-party or anti-Mao authors were also severely criticised, whereas cultural and literary institutes were closed during the Cultural Revolution. The whole Chinese literary world would also fall under state control following the wanton large-scale destruction of culture. [12]

10 Chen, *Do the Heavens Know that the People are Sick?*, 106.

11 R. Keith Schoppa, *Revolution and Its Past: Identities and Change in Modern Chinese History* (Upper Saddle River, N.J: Pearson Prentice Hall, 2006), 349.; Schoppa, *The Columbia Guide to Modern Chinese History*, p. 193.

12 Fokkema, *Report from Peking*, 154-155.

Within ten years of the Cultural Revolution, Chinese literature had essentially become communist propaganda. As communist literature took inspiration from Marxist literature, the language of communist literature started to differ from literature before 1949. It would inhibit individual expressions in favour of a homogeneous writing style. This type of official literature has been dubbed "Maoist literature"—a collectively written body of work that consists of a single voice.

When Mao Zedong died in 1976, the Cultural Revolution ended. Deng Xiaoping's "Economic Reforms" brought China into a new era; Chinese literature did not have to conform to ideology any longer. While this opened the possibility for new ways of expressions, many authors were slow to adapt to their "newfound freedoms." After experiencing such a long period of creative restrictions, it took many years before they would write more freely. It is not entirely inappropriate to assert that Chinese authors have remained relatively conservative and uncontroversial in the immediate post-Cultural Revolution period. The majority of literary critics still viewed literature through the lens of Maoism and would often demand that literature should hold a "correct" value-system and maintain the "traditions" of communist literature.

Several literary trends began to develop in Chinese literature following re-established contacts with the west. The "Scar Literature" that looked back at the physical and mental suffering of the Cultural Revolution came first in 1977. From 1979 on, other types of literature gained in popularity and the subject matter was also not limited to the Cultural Revolution anymore. Many "modern" authors began to deviate from "Maoist literature" while seeking new subject matters. They attempted to "experiment" with literature through its content and language. Authors who were labelled "rightist" were rehabilitated, and the aesthetics of literature started to become more important than their political aspect.[13] Publishing houses also started to think about market economics. Nevertheless, there were still several campaigns in the post-Cultural Revolution period that tried to reign in the authors.

Those are the "Anti-Spiritual Pollution Campaign" (1983-84) and the "Anti-Bourgeois Liberalisation Campaign" (1986-87). These two campaigns were primarily aimed at halting the "harmful" western influence that had been leaking into China since the Economic Reforms. Furthermore, following the crackdown on student protesters on Tiananmen Square, June fourth 1989, a considerable amount of authors and poets had to leave the country and start their lives anew abroad.[14]

After the "Tiananmen-incident," the party slowly began to tighten its control over the nation again. This has led to the present situation in the literature and publication domain of China.

13 Idema and Haft, *Chinese letterkunde*, 284-285; 287-288.

14 Leenhouts, *Chinese literatuur van nu*, 183; 187; 151-165.

/ KEY CONCEPTS OF CHINESE CENSORSHIP

_ Censorship
If authors want to publish a piece of literature in China, then they will face the censorship system sooner or later. What does censorship entail? Censorship often means that "an individual or a group of people use a certain way to hinder the expression of thoughts, feelings or religious views of others." The government normally forms the censoring body; however, schools; churches or even companies can use some form of censorship. Censorship is certainly not unique to China; it is also a frequent occurrence in the west. A contemporary example would be the United States after 9/11, where discussions related to religion were heavily censored. Furthermore, in the Netherlands—the country where I reside in—topics pertaining to the royal house will also be monitored.

_ The forms of censorship
There are mainly two kinds of direct censorship methods. The first is ex-ante censoring. This means that publications are censored before they are printed or released to the public. The other kind of censoring is called ex-post censoring. This means that the censorship takes place after a work or publication has been released to the public. This often means issuing a ban or prohibition on the work in question. These two kind of censorships are called external censorship—as opposed to internal or self-censorship—as it is enforced by a third party.

_ Self-censorship and vague laws
Censorship in China is significantly less systematised than the censorship system in the former Soviet Union.

The Chinese state—and the party—have significantly relaxed its grip on the publication industry since the Economic Reforms. It has since then become virtually impossible for the state apparatus to check every single publication for bad elements. This certainly does not mean that authors are able to write and express everything they want.

Authors still to need avoid sensitive topics and taboos; they also need to consider the fact that their work cannot clash with national ideologies. The state accomplishes this by using a psychological kind of censorship.

The government will stipulate general publication guidelines and the possible punishments for violating these guidelines. However, these guidelines are extremely vague. The state stipulates that the following guidelines can appear as themes in literary works:

"China has shown its heroic spirit during the Korean war";
"The plentiful yields of the Great Leap Forward have helped with the development of Tibet";
"The crimes of the Gang of Four";
"The modernisation of agriculture, industry, defence and science";
"The Chinese ethnic minorities have the most representative moral values"; "The poor human rights situation in the United States."

Not only do these guidelines lack any kind of explanation, there is also the existence of taboo topics. The state distributes a list of sensitive keywords and topics each year. The content of this list depends on national and social events. Although the majority of these keywords change, some are sure to remain on the list indefinitely, and the premise always remains the same: "never oppose or question the leadership of the Communist Party of China and its policies." The taboo list of August 2001 contains the following blacklisted topics:

_ Invalidating the leading position of Marxism, Mao Zedong Thought or Deng Xiaoping Theory;
_ Resisting the leadership of the Communist Party of China and its guidance;
_ Leaking classified information and bringing harm to national security and interests;
_ Resisting party policy related to ethnic minorities and religion, national integrity and social harmony;
_ Topics that can instigate murder, violence, obscenity, superstition or pseudo-science;
_ Spreading rumours or fake news that disrupt the normal proceedings of the party and the state.

The same level of ambiguity also lies within the legal framework of China. The Constitution of China, on the one hand, guarantees certain civil freedoms through articles 35 and 47.

Article 35:
"Citizens of the People's Republic of China enjoy freedom of speech, of the press, of assembly, of association, of procession and of demonstration."

Article 47:
"Citizens of the People's Republic of China have the freedom to engage in scientific research, literary and artistic creation and other cultural pursuits."

Article 51 and 53, on the other hand, respectively note that Chinese citizens have the freedom of expression, on the basis that this does not "infringe upon national interests." However, the constitution does not define the meaning of "national interests." This kind of ambiguity in the wording means that power holders have the flexibility to mark practically any kind of article or text as harmful to national interests whenever and wherever they want. They have essentially free reign to unleash the full might of the state in order to dispose of "harmful influences."

Authors need to judge on an ad-hoc basis whether or their work infringes on taboo topics or even national interests. Going against national guidelines will cause an immediate prohibition of the publication and can even lead to criminal prosecution. Judging what kind of content can pass the examination of the censors has become an uncertain guessing game. This intentional lack of clarity is meant to promote self-censorship, as authors need to constantly worry about the political impact of their works. This anxiety in turn causes authors to restrict themselves in their writing. Self-censorship is difficult to verify as it usually takes place on a subconscious level. The fact that many authors have given up writing after the establishment of the People's Republic of China probably says enough about the efficacy of the censorship system. Vague guidelines coupled with harsh punishments are powerful deterrents, to dissuade authors from going against the party line. Authors have essentially become their own censors.

_ Some important organisations and institutions
In China, there are essentially two entities involved with deciding the policy direction of literature, namely the Communist Party of China and the Chinese government. They have their own respective institutions and methods to control the publication sector.

Within the Chinese government—or officially known as the "State Council"—there are multiple departments involved with the management of a specific part of the publication sector. Each department has their role and responsibilities for different kinds of media. The "General Administration of Press and Publication" (GAPP) is responsible for administrating print media, such as magazines and books.

The "Central Propaganda Department" of the communist party is in charge of the cultural guidelines for the state. The Propaganda Department works together with the State Council behind closed-doors. All information that goes to the state will also be diverted to the Propaganda Department. The Propaganda Department ensures that the media and publication sector adhere to party guidelines and ideology.

The various department and institutes of the state and the party are intricately interwoven with each other. The censorship system relies on this very institutional foundation.

The Propaganda Department regularly convenes meetings on national and local levels to relay new policy directions. This ensures that a coherent policy is in place on a national level.

/ CHAPTER 1
INDEPENDENT AUTHORS

/ YE FU

_First encounters

Ye Fu and I met each other on June 2012. Ye Fu received an invitation from the Nederlands Letterenfonds (Dutch Foundation for Literature) to stay several months in Amsterdam as a writer-in-residence. Back then, I was the translator at a meeting between the chairman of the foundation and Ye Fu. His experiences and stories about China had left me speechless at the dinner table. A year later, I immediately wrote down Ye Fu's name on my list of interview candidates. Soon afterwards, I received news that Ye Fu would be visiting Cologne and I set my mind on interviewing him face-to-face. Before long, we met up at the Cologne Cathedral.

I vividly remember that I could not help but be captivated by the high ceilings of the cathedral while I was thinking to myself that the splendour of the ceilings almost induced a sense of vertigo. At that moment, the thunderous voice of Ye Fu suddenly resounded throughout the cathedral. As if being struck by lightning, he brought me back to my senses. With a single word, he had my full attention. Just like I remember him from our previous meeting, he was dressed casually, while his face carried a friendly smile. As soon as we sat down at the cafe down the street, Ye Fu got straight to the point:

"You can ask me anything, there is no need to hold back on my account." Thus, I started the interview.

Ye Fu—also known as "Ye Fu the Tujia"—was born as Zheng Shiping (1962). Zheng grew up in the autonomous prefecture of Enshi, Hubei province, home of the Tujia and Miao ethnic minority groups of China. Several of his well-known works are MOTHER ON THE RIVER; MY FATHER'S WAR; SAMSARA: AN ELEGY; TO WHERE HOME MAY BE; and INVISIBLE RIVERS. His book MOTHER ON THE RIVER won a prize in the category of "best non-fiction literature" at the 2010 Taipei International Book Exhibition; therefore, becoming the first author from China to ever win this prize. Moreover, he is proficient in various literary styles and has written in all kinds of genres, such as poems, prose, novels, dramas, non-fiction literature and screenplays. In short, the author Ye Fu—and his work—arguably hold a significant place in contemporary Chinese literature.

Zheng Shiping enrolled in the literature department at the Hubei Institute for Nationalities in 1978. The next year he started composing poetry. Zheng has harboured dreams of becoming an author since childhood. Fuelled by his dream, he became a lively poetry aficionado in college. When Zheng returned home in 1982, he started the "Poetry Society of Jujube Peelers" and began using his pen name "Ye Fu" (literally "The Wild Man"). He published his first poems in influential poetry magazines such as *Yangtze Literature* and *Xing Xing* in the period 1982-83. Furthermore, the first underground publication of the poetry anthology *Night Howl of the Wolves* came into being under the responsibility of Ye Fu in 1985.

The 1980s was a period of turbulence for underground poets. Many underground poets did not publish in mainstream magazines, as official publications were relatively conservative. To put it more bluntly, regardless of the aesthetics, theme or style of the underground poets, the magazines rejected every aspect of their boisterous poetry. Driven by their rebellious spirit, the poets simply printed their own magazine, with their poetry filling the bulk of the pages.

_ From poet to dissident and then back to being author

Ye Fu worked for the police in 1988; however, he abandoned his post when the protest at Tiananmen Square erupted in 1989. In the aftermath of the protest, the state suspected Ye Fu of having participated in the Tiananmen Square incident and sentenced him in 1990 to six years in prison for "leaking state secrets." His father died of cancer while Ye Fu was serving his sentence. He left prison in 1995, after he received a reduced sentence. Unable to bear with their situation any longer, his mother committed suicide. Left alone without any relatives, Ye Fu decided to leave for Beijing and founded a private book company. However, his passion for writing did not diminish in prison. After the things that had happened to him and his family, he simply harboured too many things within his being that needed an outlet. Should he refrain from writing it down on paper, it is likely that he would die full of regret and remorse. Thus, in 2006, he finally decided to abandon everything else in order to pursue his dream of writing once more.

There is a saying about Ye Fu, namely that his work will fill his readers with a sense of tremendous horror. His twenty thousand-word essay "Requiem for a Landlord," for example, tells the family history of his father and its fall and devastation. Because Ye Fu's grandfather was a landlord, he was tortured to death during the agricultural collectivisation movement in 1951-53. Even his uncle, who was a senior member of the communist party, could not escape from prosecution. He also died during the reforms. Meanwhile, the state sentenced his second uncle to hard labour. He went on to work on the farms for more than thirty years. His uncles' wives decided to hang themselves as a result of all this misfortune.

Ye Fu has written about these painful life events, because he wanted to convey the message that the Chinese rural gentry had once carried the spirit of Chinese culture. However, the land reforms have totally destroyed the very embodiment of this spirit. This is what Ye Fu has exposed to his readers—the horrible truth of this period in Chinese history.

When he published his essay on the Internet, his story attracted a delirious amount of readers before the censors removed it. He, subsequently, collected an edited version of the essay in the essay-bundle SAMSARA: AN ELEGY. However, in spite of his efforts, the censors still banned the whole book because of the included essay.

_An oblique censorship system

In spite of the ban on his underground magazine, books and work, Ye Fu has a relatively comfortable life, free of worries. The truth of the matter is that, as an independent writer, you can keep writing as long as you do not participate in any groups or collective action or violate any kind of principle. The censorship system in China has another interesting phenomenon: censors do not re-examine republications of books, if not the examination will not be as strict as before. This is a matter of cost; if every publication and republication needed an examination, there will not be enough manpower and capital. There are some authors who make use of this fact by simply adding in the republication an "extra chapter" that incidentally went "missing" during the initial print.

Even when the censors have banned your book, as long as you change the title and make appropriate adjustments to the content, the book can be republished anytime later. Ye Fu's illustrates this with the work—TO WHERE HOME MAY BE. This collection of essays is actually the revised version of SAMSARA: AN ELEGY. After changing the book title and some of the book chapters, Ye Fu re-introduced the book to the Chinese audience. The book went on to become a commercial success and even ended up on several top-10 recommendations lists in 2012. While the publisher received a serious warning for the publication, it never led to a ban. Ye Fu suspects that the book has become too well-known to the public; therefore, its influence exceeded the control of the state censors. The publisher resisted pressure, and continued to market the book and kept pushing sales. However, in spite of their success, the publisher—in light of another severe warning—ended up passing on the publication rights of Ye Fu's next work BESIDES RIVERS AND LAKES. Ye Fu regardlessly released the book through another publisher one year later. A ban never came and the book went on to enjoy great sales. Although Ye Fu is grateful for this unexpected windfall, it also left him with many questions:

"What kind of book will lead to a ban?" And what constitutes an actual ban?

Many Chinese authors have racked their brains over these same questions, yet a definite answer remains to be found.

_ The three examinations

Each year, the General Administration of Press and Publication (GAPP)—the government body responsible for censoring publications—releases a list to each news agency that contains a list of blacklisted keywords. The GAPP releases at least thirty of these lists on a yearly basis, frequently changing the content of the list in order to accurately reflect the ever-changing political situation. Some sensitive keywords—such as "Tiananmen Square"—remain on the list indefinitely. Some blacklisted keywords may cover a wide range of topics, whereas the descriptions of others keywords are vague sometimes. This makes it hard to define a clear boundary on what is acceptable—and what is not; thus making the censorship system even harder to understand than it already is.

Ye Fu is well-acquainted with the intricacies of the censorship system, both as an author and as the owner of a private book company. Especially the approval process of a book is an area where he has considerable knowledge on. "The first step in the production phase of a book," as he related to me, "is for the publisher to hand in a book proposal of their solicited works to the local office of the GAPP." This proposal contains a detailed report on the contracted author and the book outline. During this initial stage of the examination, the GAPP will inevitably reject a certain amount of book proposals. However, it is practically impossible for the GAPP to have a detailed understanding of each and every proposal; hence, it will pass the examination of individual cases on to the publishing house. Thus, the examination process will shift to another process colloquially known as "the three examinations," which denotes a three-pronged examination. The managing editor is the first examiner of the manuscript. The second examiner is the editorial board. The third examiner is the editor-in-chief. The GAPP will only issue a book identification number after these three layers of examination have approved the manuscript. Publishing houses need these identification numbers, because without one they will not able to officially release the book on the domestic market.

China is to all intents and purposes still a planned economy; therefore, confiscating the book identification number is a relatively "effective" method for enforcing a ban. The General Administration issues a set amount of identification numbers for publishers on a yearly basis. The GAPP determines this quota on the basis of the size, speciality and portfolio of the publishing house. Losing one identification number due to a ban effectively means missing out on an important source of revenue. The book company of Ye Fu is not able to publish any books. For that reason his company can only officially involve itself with the production of books, such as soliciting manuscripts and editing. When it comes down to getting an identification number and publishing the book itself, he will need to rely on an official publishing house.

Ye Fu spoke from experience when he stated that the style of the work is an important factor for a ban. If you were to write a history book describing the decade in which the Cultural Revolution took place, than your book would have zero chances at publication.

Should you use the Cultural Revolution as the backdrop for your novel instead, it would technically still qualify for a ban, but it would not be unthinkable for the Chinese public to read your book at some time in the future. Furthermore, sensitive pieces of work will have greater chances of seeing publication in the hands of capable publishers and editors, who are willing to fight on behalf of their authors. Nevertheless, when a book proves too influential—in other words, moving too far from the political line of the Chinese Communist Party—it will risk a ban. If that were to happen, the one facing the consequences will not only be the author, but also the people involved with the book publication. The subsequent punishment can range from disciplinary actions, such as demotions on administrative or party levels, to more extreme measures such as capital punishment. Naturally, the most straightforward measure would be to fire the responsible editor and to disband the publishing house.

_ Publishing, censoring and self-censorship

Ye Fu does not like to call himself an author. He tends to call himself a "writer with freedom." When he told me this, I could not help but ask him back whether there exists true creative freedom in present-day China. Ye Fu agrees that authors will undoubtedly restrain their own writing if they want to release their book for the domestic market. Things that they really want to write will remain unwritten. However, there are more options today compared to ten years ago. Not only can you publish on the Internet, but being able to publish overseas, such as in Hong Kong or Taiwan, has allowed for more creative freedom for writers in China. All authors can publish overseas if they are not political dissidents. A literary novel, for example, has good chances of getting publication in Hong Kong and Taiwan. Nevertheless, this option is not viable for everyone. If you are part of the "Chinese Writers' Association," you are writing on government sponsorship, and therefore, subjected to a different standard. Should you choose to publish your work through one of the aforementioned options, then your work cannot stray too far from the political line, or else it will influence your future professional career in China.

On the topic of state-employed authors, Ye Fu feels that there is no lack of talented writers with outstanding artistic achievements. It is only natural for them to feel apprehensive about the situation in China, because they exist within the system.

For example, Mo Yan—laureate of the Nobel Prize of Literature in 2012 and member of the Chinese Writers' Association—once told a journalist, who asked him about creative freedom in China, that the present situation is already much better than thirty years ago. Ye Fu ostensibly agrees with Mo Yan in noting that the present situation is better than the Cultural Revolution. However, he sardonically concludes that authors still need to impose strict self-censorship on their work. China has too many areas that still need improvement. Ye Fu spoke in an earnest manner when he remarked that people tend to have a self-loathing, self-abased side. People will try to evade taboos and sensitive topics even on the Internet, which is comparatively free in China. It goes without saying that when you break a taboo in China, you could risk personal danger and lose all your individual freedom. In the face of such dire consequences, people tend to circumscribe themselves: you will put a restriction on the things you can write about, and tacitly comply with what must remain unspoken, unwritten and untouched.

_ Cruel to be kind

Living in relative comfort, the present Ye Fu could decide not to trouble himself anymore with magnanimous things, such as caring for "the truth" and revealing it at the risk of his own personal well-being. For all he cares, he could be living his life in peace and quiet. Regardless, Ye Fu is a man of letters. Just like the adage "the more you love, the harsher you need to be," he earnestly wants to continue influencing people through his work, while fostering their historical awareness. One generation has already shed too much blood, whereas he personally does not want to leave another bloodshed world for his children or their descendants. Giving up at the halfway-mark would simply be the selfish thing to do; however, Ye Fu is all but a selfish man.

/ RAN YUNFEI

_ Social activist and author

I met Ran Yunfei at an art festival co-organised by Cologne's "Academy of the Arts of the World" and the "Cologne Literature House." The theme "Unheard China: a critical dialogue" covered discussions such as Chinese historical facts (i.e. politically sensitive events) and the domestic situation (e.g. censorship of printed and Internet media; creative freedom for authors). The panel was able to freely discuss these topics with the gathered public. Moreover, when it comes to talking about freedom and democracy in China, no one is more qualified than Ran Yunfei—social activist and author.

The first time I have heard of Ran Yunfei was not from his publications; it was from the news of his arrest in 2011 by the Sichuan police department. His call for a "Jasmine Revolution"—in other words a plea for freedom and democracy—caused him to subsequently be charged with the crime of "inciting subversion of state power." Due to insufficient evidence, the state released Ran Yunfei from detention six months later. Ran promptly returned to his home in Chengdu, Sichuan province. However, that was not the first time he had participated in a movement: during the Wenchuan earthquake in May 2008, he organised and participated in the Sichuan Earthquake relief aid event held by bulldog.cn—a Chinese political website. In December that year, he was among those who signed "Charter 08"; a manifesto calling for democratic reforms in China. And in January 2009, he signed an open letter called "Boycott China Central Television, Resist Brainwashing" in order to protest the propaganda-like broadcasting of state television.

Ran Yunfei has a strong interest in the protection of liberal rights and historical issues—one of his personal passions. The very prolific nature of his activities tends to attract national attention, which subsequently often leads him to face the "repercussions" of his actions. This can range from the seemingly-insignificant, such as blocking access to his personal blog; to the severe, such as imprisonment. Furthermore, he is also an author.

A long-time resident of Chengdu, Ran Yunfei (1965) was born in Youyang County, Chongqing municipality. He graduated in 1987 from the literature department of Sichuan University. His stories frequently focus on the malpractices found in contemporary Chinese society. Some of his signature works are MALADY: CRISIS AND CRITICISMS OF THE CHINESE EDUCATIONAL SYSTEM; and RAT RACE TOWARDS AN EMPIRE OF IDIOTS. As for historical expositions, he has written EXILE OF THE HANDWRITTEN MANUSCRIPT; and THE LUNG OF OLD SICHUAN: CHRONICLES

OF THE TEMPLE OF GREAT COMPASSION. The wide scope of his work, combined with his infatuation with Tang-era poems and Zhuangzi—one of China's greatest philosophers—truly make Ran Yunfei a well-rounded polymath in Chinese literature.

_ Expressing gratitude for publication

It is probably easy to imagine the difficulty for Ran Yunfei to publish any kind of "critical" book in a country with strict censorship. Take his book RAT RACE TOWARDS AN EMPIRE OF IDIOTS for example; several publishers had refused to publish the book because they considered the content too sensitive for publication.

RAT RACE TOWARDS AN EMPIRE OF IDIOTS contains selected essays of Ran Yunfei written since 1998. Space limitations were one reason in opting for a "selected-works"-format. The other reason was certain "problems" with the content. One particular book segment saw the most edits, namely "The Pitiful Chinese Education." It contained essays such as the polemical "Mandatory Education is the Biggest Lie of China" and "The Chinese Educational System Needs Reform" These essays would probably not pass the official examination if Ran did not alter them. He also needed to delete whole treatises on Chinese history, such as "The Modern History China needs." The "problem" with these articles is that they stimulate critical thinking and invite public scrutiny—things that inherently threaten the much-vaunted "social stability" of the political establishment.

After these edits, the book could finally be published through Huacheng Publishing (Guangzhou) in February 2008. Although he had to alter his content, Ran Yunfei still voiced his thanks to the publisher for actually publishing the book.

_ From censorship to freedom of expression

The aforementioned examples illustrate what limit there is on the freedom of expression in China. Ran Yunfei has to work in such an environment as an author. Freedom and limitation evidently go hand-in-hand with each other, but the real problem is the degree that is applied. Ran often thinks to himself that it would be better, if he could just write the things he wants to write about, without any kind of restriction. However, reality often runs counter to what one desires it to be.

Ran argues that freedom of expression is not something that only applies to authors. It is something where everyone has a stake in it. Should we lose our freedom of expression, not only will it decrease our forms of expression, we will also be unable to stop any further infringement upon our basic rights. Conversely, when there is freedom of expression, it will subsequently promote independent and rational thought. The latter situation is exactly what the Communist Party of China wants to prevent. Should the Chinese people one day become cognisant of the facts that the party has kept from them, then the party would lose influence and the people might rebel against its authority. The consequences would be downright disastrous for the party.

Freedom of expression and independent thought should not be things that are conditionally given at the behest of others. Should it be given on a conditional basis, then there is no knowing when it will be taken away. That is why these two basic needs should be an inalienable right. However, Ran Yunfei has found out that few people are willing to fight for these rights in China. Some of them are not even conscious of it, while others have plainly given up on it. The people belonging to the latter category are probably "hedging their bets" against the state. Most people will adopt a principle of see no-evil, hear no-evil and speak no-evil when confronted with this issue. In his opinion, this is equal to being complicit in a "silent conspiracy."

It can be likened to the way history is treated in China: each and every person knows the difference between right and wrong, yet everyone acts as if they are ignorant when facing the truth, reluctant to raise a voice. They are in a rat-race towards stupidity: a competition being the best at acting like a fool while pretending to look the other way around.

Nevertheless, there may be many reasons for not breaking the silence, especially when there are potential ramifications to your family, your friends and yourself. The amount of people participating in this silent conspiracy keeps growing with each day as a consequence. Should this continue in this manner, then it will grow increasingly more difficult to break the silence. Should you speak the naked truth in this kind of situation, then you will only attract the anger and castigation of the public.

_Between a rock and a hard place

This "silent conspiracy" is actually a fitting description for the Chinese literature world. Chinese authors, especially the ones working within the official circuit, constantly need to calculate the risk for writing honestly. This often leads to a cautionary attitude where everyone averts their gaze in silence and where they only make a passing acknowledgement to the truth. At best, they will treat it merely as a curiosity, a joke or just a run-of-the mill event, just so their work can amuse the political establishment, entertain the readers and ultimately to protect themselves.

There are some people who defend the current system in order to protect their own interests. They claim that censorship actually benefits creativity and they argue for further political involvement with the literary profession. However, literature cannot only focus on the positive sides of life. Authors also need to write about the negative aspects of historical periods and the darkness of humans in order for people to properly reflect on reality. Many state-employed authors have been able to write about these things in spite of censorship.

However, they tend to bend and distort facts in such way that their work is ultimately too far removed from reality.

This begs the question of what criteria are important for censors: could it be that censors only care about the theme and content? Or are there other factors? Based on his experiences and those of his friends, Ran Yunfei told me that the censors will also take the personal background of the author into account. If the author has a "previous offence" of defying official discourse, it is quite likely that the author will either risk censorship or a ban, if not receive unfair treatment. Furthermore, if there are authors who write something similar to the work of a persecuted author, their work will also be banned regardless of the content. However, when this concerns a writer who has some influence within the official writer's circuit, the censor will reconsider the circumstances and refrain from punishing too harshly, even if the concerned work is somewhat out of line.

The genre or style is also an important factor. If it is non-fiction literature—such as biographies, prose, or memoirs—than it is quite likely that the book will not pass examination. However—as mentioned by Ye Fu—if the work is fiction, such as a novel, it is more likely for the book to escape censorship. Ran explains this as follows:

"Firstly, the work is fictional; therefore the story arguably does not take place in the real world. Secondly, a novel can hide insinuations or critiques in obscure metaphors in order to elude the censors. That is why it can be said that Chinese censorship is flexible, with no absolute standards, nor any clearly defined rules to refer to."

Nevertheless, there are some things that can never appear in a novel, such as the Tiananmen-incident. If there is even the slightest mention of it in a book manuscript, the whole publication process might as well be abandoned immediately. The Chinese government tends to label these types of historical events as "political disturbances." For example, the Anti-Rightist Movement of 1957 and the Cultural Revolution are such sensitive events. If you do not carefully approach these events in your book, you will simply risk immediate censorship. The same level of cautiousness applies to academics—they also need to hide their work behind a veil of obscurity.
Ran Yunfei does not think that the Chinese Communist Party really wants to prevent authors from writing. Strategically speaking, the policy is to instil self-censorship, but only to the extent that authors will refrain from bringing sensitive issues into the public. The few who are willing to break the "silent conspiracy" will only receive the rebuttal and mockery of society. Furthermore, speaking up might cause a strain in their personal relations, and hamper them in their own personal lives. Many will ask the following question when they are faced with such adversity:

"Being left wretched and disappointed, is there a point to being an author anymore?"

If they did not bother with such "lofty goals"—and just started a small business instead—their lives would probably have been better in general. It is this realisation that has led many people, at their wit's end, to just give up. This is exactly the desired goal of the system: in order to halt any resistance against the government, it pushes defiant authors to the brink of desolation and destroys their will to continue writing.

_ No greater joy than fighting censorship

Having sparred with censors for such a long time, Ran Yunfei has accrued ample experience in this cat-and-mouse game. During the interview, he brought up a quantitative method for deciding the likelihood of being censored.

"If you want to understand the sensitive nature of a certain event or person, you tally the occurrences of that name in the media. If the official media lack even the least bit of slander of said name, then this indicates that there is a powerful restriction in place. However, if state media are openly slandering a person, this actually means that the name is in fact not very sensitive at all. In that case, we can surmise that there is no problem with mentioning the name in public, nor will there be any repercussions attached to it."

As an example, Ran Yunfei mentions Liu Xiaobo—the first Chinese recipient of the Peace Nobel prize, and political prisoner in China:

"His name appears only once in the *Global Daily* [an official state newspaper]; thus, you should be careful to avoid mentioning his name or things associated with him. Otherwise, it is quite likely that you will be censored."

Towards the end of our interview, Ran Yunfei used the following comparison that thoroughly explains the way the system works. Imagine that the censorship system is like a valve above a water reservoir. The water is information; the flow rate is the distribution speed of the information; and the water amount in the reservoir indicates public awareness. These three things are all under the control of the government: it can decide whether to open or close the source of information; where the information will flow to; and how much of the information is publicly available; thus, firmly controlling public discourse and independent thought. They also have dikes in place in the form of active censorship to stem the tide of information after it gets out in the public. The Chinese government is ultimately the one who decides how information is going to flow to the people, from beginning to end.

It can be said that each and every person in China shares an instituted fear of the system. Nevertheless, there are still people like Ran Yunfei who are able to turn their fear into courage. Driven by a desire to freely express themselves, and to have democracy and universal freedom in China one day, they continue to devote their whole being to bringing the realisation of these goals closer each day.

/ MIAN MIAN

_ The unknown famous author

I met Mian Mian in the Netherlands at the 2011 Amsterdam book fair "Manuscripta." At the time, the Netherlands was the host country for the 2011 Beijing International Book Fair. In order to further promote Chinese-Dutch culture exchanges, the Nederlands Letterenfonds (Dutch Foundation for Literature) invited two Chinese authors to participate in their writers-in-residence program. One of them was Mian Mian.

I remember I was twenty-five at the time and it was the first time I have ever heard of the author Mian Mian. You can probably imagine my surprise when my colleague at the foundation told me she is a long well-known Chinese author in America and Europe—especially in France. I felt bewildered as I—as a Chinese—have never heard or seen any mention of such an internationally renowned author in China. In fact, why has she never released any books domestically? And how was her work introduced to the international market? What did she write that made her suddenly become famous in the west?

As these questions fed my curiosity, I set out to find more about this person.

Therefore, I searched the Internet and found out that—apart from being an author—she also plays music, holds book-reading events, acts in films and regularly goes abroad to promote her work. There was one interesting titbit to her personal history: not only are her books blacklisted in China, she also hangs out in the underground music scene, holds book-reading events about banned books, and she acts in art house cinema. That explains why the name "Mian Mian" has remained relatively obscure in China; the censors would not allow it to be otherwise.

As I investigated the reason behind the ban, I have written her experiences with censorship down in this chapter.

_ From childhood infamy to international fame

Born as Wang Xin (1970) in Shanghai, Mian Mian started composing poetry and short stories from the age of sixteen. Her ambition started out simple: writing was a way for self-expression, a way for her to look cool and stand out in a crowd. Mian Mian was a troublemaker as a child, but she was calm most of the time, and would pass off as a silent child. Whenever there was an opportunity, she would be reading books. However, when she turned seventeen, Mian Mian decided to quit high school. From then on, until the age of twenty-five, her life would turn itself upside down. Mian Mian would move back-and-forth in South-China, hopping from city to city, such as Guangzhou, Shenzhen and Hong Kong.

In 1997, New Century Press (Hong Kong) published an overseas edition of LA LA LA—her first collected works. CANDY came out three years later. To date CANDY remains her most famous work. The Hong Kong publication of this book was an important factor for paving the road to international success: CANDY was translated in fifteen languages, and saw publication in countries, such as the Netherlands, Brazil, France, Germany, Greece, Italy, Portugal, Spain and the United States. The thorny path that led to the huge success of CANDY will be discussed in a later section.

Her next work PANDA SEX came four years after CANDY. Other (yet to be translated) works include SOCIAL DANCE; EVERY GOOD CHILD DESERVES TO EAT CANDY; YOUR NIGHT IS MY DAY; INFAMOUS; RISING TO HEAVEN FROM TOMORROW'S MELANCHOLY. Her work often concerns the lives of young Chinese, with their stories often reflecting the changes in contemporary China. Although Mian Mian's work is often dark and decadent, it is often ripe with emotion and overflowing with passion.

_ Bogged down in censorship

From the moment when she started writing, Mian Mian has continued to spar with censorship. When Yunnan Publishing planned to release LA LA LA for domestic release in 1999, the newly printed books were met with an immediate ban. In 2000, Shanhua Publishing also received a ban for EVERY GOOD CHILD DESERVES TO EAT CANDY. Her novel CANDY, which was published four months earlier in that year, also received a nationwide ban. On that same day, the General Administration of Press and Publication issued a document announcing a moratorium on all news related to Mian Mian. From that moment onward, it was forbidden to talk about Mian Mian or discuss her work in China.

The beginning of her troubles with censorship did not start in 1999. Acute readers might notice that a substantial amount of time had passed between her first publication in 1997 and when she started writing in 1987. This could partly be attributed to her lifestyle at the time—underground parties and drug use certainly did not promote a strict work ethic—but the deciding factor was the strict publication rules in China.

Back in March 1987, Mian Mian hoped to have her story accepted in Shanghai Literature—a publication dedicated to short stories. The editor at the time soon dashed the hopes of a sixteen year old when he did not want to deal with the backlash of publishing a story that involved a high school suicide. Like this, the debut work of Mian

Mian missed out on its publication. From then on out, Mian Mian met one problem after another and before she knew it, ten years had passed.

_ A sensation caused by CANDY

Among her banned work, CANDY is arguably the most influential. Several domestic publishers passed on the opportunity to publish her book before *Harvest*—one of China's premier literary journals—took a risk on it. The publication even ended up at a few bestsellers' sections before the censors pulled it from the bookstores.

At the time, the Chinese were steadily increasing their Internet usage. A radical group of authors—most notably female authors—started tearing away at the "Berlin Wall" in Chinese literature in an attempt to break with its tradition and conventions. CANDY was like a Molotov cocktail that lit the whole Chinese literary scene on fire.

CANDY is about a girl, who is a high-school dropout and lives with her parents. All her friends share the same situation as her. They tend to live lavishly, unrestrained, while indulging in their wants and desires. They experiment with drugs, sex and same-sex relationships; and frequent discos, bars and the drug rehabilitation clinic. Sinking in the deepest of pleasures, they are unable to free themselves from such a life of decadence. They only know how to crash and burn through their youth.

As CANDY also featured candid descriptions of sexual relationships, the book quickly attracted the attention of the censors. Four months later CANDY disappeared along with its author from public eye. At first sight, one might think that the book is singled out for typical reasons such as vulgarity, lack of morals and its so-called "harmful influence on the youth." In reality, the GAPP did hesitate when considering the ban. Back when the book was still under review, Mian Mian actually received a telephone call on a Friday notifying her that no ban will follow. However, the following Monday, news agencies received a notice by facsimile, expressly forbidding each and every media outlet in the nation from ever discussing Mian Mian and her works.

The prohibition closed the doors for Mian Mian's writing existence in China; however, as if the fates had something else in store for her, the ban opened a window of opportunity for her international career. Following the ban, overseas publishers were clamouring at her doorsteps to publish CANDY. Serendipitously, CANDY rose from blacklisted publication to international bestseller as a result. On the domestic side, the state prohibition on CANDY did not go unnoticed. Many readers, who have only heard of Mian Mian in passing, started to read her work out of curiosity. Even though CANDY disappeared from the bookstore shelves, readers could still read the book on the Internet or through various other means. The state censors tolerated this as long as the book was not published or sold in an overtly public manner. Every now and then, CANDY would just "coincidentally" show up for sale in China.

_ Beyond CANDY

Graphic descriptions of sexuality or so-called "vulgar" themes certainly may have triggered the ban; however, that is just one small aspect of the story. CANDY is first and foremost a love story, but to really do justice to the book, you also need to understand the background of the story.

The narrative spans the period 1989-99, a period when China is undergoing a great transformation. During the 1990s, China is rapidly transforming from a plan economy to a market economy. Faced with enormous changes and unfamiliar concepts—such as consumerism—a general sense of loss and disappointment pervaded through the younger generation. The author channels this through her male lead—Saining—whose life history is like an analogue to Chinese society.

Saining comes from a place in South-China that has the early makings of a "modern" city. When he just arrived at Beijing, the local art scene compels Saining to use the (communist) words "sense of duty" and "collectivism" to describe its atmosphere. If you were to compare Beijing and South-China back then, the disparity would be enormous. Beijing stood symbol for the very success of the communist revolution, whereas the liberal south has historically been exposed to western culture. In Beijing you could linger around in the ideals of communist fervour, but this mentality was steadily eroding away in the south. Shenzhen in Southern China was transforming from a small fishing village into a big commercial hub. It was a test bed for the economic reforms of Deng Xiaoping; furthermore, it was a prototype for future Chinese cities; and it was a place where China could have its first taste of consumerism.

The book reflects this cultural gap in the music values of Saining and his friend Sanmao. Sanmao, on the one hand, bears the essence of the revolutionary idealist. He feels a sense of duty towards music, something solemn that is able to change life and destiny. Saining, on the other hand, does not plays music out of duty, but simply because he likes it.

The personal circumstances of Saining have shaped these values: his parents were accused of political crimes during the Cultural Revolution. Saining grew under constant anxiety as he grew in the rural parts of North-west China. His parents were eventually rehabilitated, but they were unable to reconcile as a family. His parents divorced and his mother moved to Japan with her new husband, while Saining followed his father to Britain.

There are several meanings reflected in the portrayal of Saining and Sanmao. Saining is a prime example of how each person and every family suffered during the Cultural Revolution. This causes Saining to feel apprehensive towards Beijing even in adulthood. He rejects and dreads anything related to politics or duty, which stems from his lingering fears of Beijing—the very bastion of Chinese politics and the symbol of communist revolution.

Sanmao—the idealist and youthful revolutionary—ends up becoming a drug addict beyond help at the end of the story. His life is a symbol for the futility of the Cultural Revolution and its eventual demise. The characterisation of Saining and Sanmao is but an example of how CANDY evokes its post-revolutionary spirit to the reader.

_ **Understanding changes in censorship with the re-release of CANDY**
More than a decade has passed since the original publication of CANDY. In 2009, CANDY was republished for the domestic market. It is uncertain when the ban was lifted on CANDY, but Mian Mian personally thinks that the state censors still consider her name and bibliography as sensitive topics.

It is possible that the current regime still rejects depictions of sex and drug abuse in books. However, China has become increasingly more liberal on these matters, as these themes have become recurring topics in Chinese literature, especially when compared to volatile topics such as the Cultural Revolution, Chinese politics and society (think for example of what Ye Fu has mentioned on this topic earlier in this chapter). Censorship has changed in the past decade in the sense that they will permit books with "low moral fibre," but as a trade-off, political content has become a no-go zone for authors. The 2009 reprint of CANDY reflects this change.

When Mian Main was interviewed for the reprint in 2009, she reservedly expressed the following statement:

"The reprint of CANDY has removed weighty content related to society. As a result, it has become more of a distilled love story. Overall, the reprint has a less heavy tone than the original work. Life in general is difficult enough already, there is no need to trouble the reader with these things. Back when I was young, I had many things to say. There were things such as love, but I also had the male lead represent the changing nation. In the new edition, the romance aspects form the highlight of the story."

Despite these changes, Mian Mian still had to wait an excruciatingly long time before official approval. The examination period took one year in total, while she had to endure unreliable publishers and constant revisions. It was one delay after another. There was even one time when Mian Mian received her manuscript back from the editor and found out it was covered in red marks. Mian Mian could only read it for ten minutes before she burst into tears.

After switching publisher and patiently waiting another half year, it finally looked as if Mian Mian could escape her censors. However, when the book came out, the publisher remained silent, and the book did not even appear on bookstore shelves.

_ The non-existent author

As for her personal feelings on the ban, Mian Mian always reminds herself that she should not treat herself as a victim, nor should anyone think that she only gained international fame because of her prohibition. If there was even the slightest chance of preventing a ban, Mian Mian would have done anything in her power to do so. Receiving a ban as a young author has caused her to be unable to publish normally or even appear in any kind of media for over a decade. She stresses that this has been an exceedingly awful situation for her.

Mian Mian notes that she has never deliberately chosen to venture into political topics for her work. She points out that the sexuality in her work is also something that has traditionally been around in Chinese literature. As a matter of fact, her writing and her personal mind-set is about breaking through convention. It is about heeding your inner self and developing social awareness. Perhaps it is because Mian Mian has this kind of distinctive and alternative awareness in her writing that naturally led her to collide with censorship.

There was one time when she tried to write an editorial under an alias, but the article was promptly censored. After changing her pen-name, the end result was still the same. Her screenplays also do not survive official examinations. It is almost an exaggeration, but wherever her name appears in China, it will almost certainly result in a ban.

There are many things Mian Mian would not say in China. She feels that there will always be CCTV cameras monitoring her nearby. Even though Mian Mian has suffered from censorship from the start of her writing career until her forties, she still hopes to have a normal publication for once. However, Mian Main is afraid that she has already become irrelevant. She states that she already lacks the ability to write something creative that is truly profound and meaningful.

Being banned for so many years, Mian Mian has given up on influencing Chinese society through her own behaviour and individual example. Writing is now just a way for self-cultivation. Nevertheless, she still hopes that her work can help her readers lessen some of the pain and anxiety caused by love. As long as she lives, Mian Mian will continue writing. After all this time, censorship has never ever made her lose her belief in writing. However, she firmly stresses that she has no personal investment in the literary world of China. This is something to be taken at face value: should anyone try to find Mian Mian through the "Chinese Writers' Association" you will not be able to find her name. Mian Mian simply does not exist in the Chinese world of literature. Despite the fact that her work is translated into fifteen different languages and read all over the world, does not change the fact that her work remains unacknowledged in China.

The only thing Mian Mian wants to do now is just to take care of her own business. She simply hopes that her writing enables her readers to find their inner self and raise their social awareness. What happens in the past stays in the past. Should her readers personally be able to find love, happiness, truth or meaning in her work, then there is nothing more that she could hope for.

/ SHI KANG

_ Bestselling author

When I was preparing my material for this chapter about Shi Kang, I read his novel LOAFING AROUND. The book left me with the impression that the author probably had his fair share of encounters with censorship. My suspicions proved right, as I found out that Shi Kang had to "begrudgingly" revise his manuscript numerous times for official approval.

Shi Kang (1968) was born and raised in Beijing. A screenwriter and an author, he started his writing career in 1993, and released his first novel in 1998. His debut LOAFING AROUND, plus his next two novels—BROKEN TO PIECES and COMPLETELY BEFUDDLED—are also known as the "Youth Trilogy." In 2007, he adapted his book STRUGGLE into a screenplay for television, which went on to become a raving success with the television audience in China. The success of the television drama and his trilogy has propelled Shi Kang into the ranks of China's top earning authors. Moreover, the film BIG SHOT'S FUNERAL, in which he shares credit as co-writer, was also a sensational success in China. Apart from his string of successes, Shi Kang has also published several essay bundles and short story collections. In spite of his accomplishment, his work remains yet to be translated into English. This chapter is about Shi Kang—one of China's bestselling authors.

_ The dawn of LOAFING AROUND

In 1998, Shi Kang debuted his coming-of-age novel LOAFING AROUND. Almost immediately, it gained widespread attention of the public. The book broke record numbers: selling over one million copies both in official and in bootlegged form, it was the bestselling novel of 1999. Seemingly each and every person was reading and talking about Shi Kang and LOAFING AROUND. His "Youth Trilogy" has since then become classics in the coming-of-age genre. It could even be argued that Shi Kang pioneered the coming-of-age genre in contemporary Chinese literature—a remarkable achievement.

Shi Kang started writing LOAFING AROUND in 1995. Back then, his screenwriting career had come to a sudden halt. This left him with much free time at hand, which he spent mostly at home. One night, Shi Kang suddenly started reminiscing about the good old times and before he knew it, he suddenly found himself writing LOAFING AROUND. Three months later he had finished his book; however, he would eventually have to wait three years before the book saw publication. From then on, Shi Kang's life as an author had begun.

LOAFING AROUND is a portrayal of the lives of young adults. The title and story of LOAFING AROUND describe their feelings of confusion and uncertainty of growing up in modern China. Narrated from a first-person point of view, the book follows the life and personal relations of the main character during college and after graduation. Shi Kang deliberately writes in an unorganised manner to accurately capture the lives of Chinese youths. This style has earned him many fans as his readers find their lives mirrored in the book.

The themes found in LOAFING AROUND are experiences that everyone can relate to, such as "starting a music band as a student to fight off the monotony of college life," "preparing for exams," "being driven by impulsiveness," before finally "becoming part of society." Shi Kang vividly details the "growing pains" associated with these experiences: becoming cynical as you grow older; being too scared to deal with the responsibilities of love; desiring escape, yet somehow wanting to belong somewhere. The male lead of the story struggles to cope with a paradoxical life that is full of tireless repetition. He finds himself "loafing around" in life and in his personal relations. And as a result of being unable to stomach his behaviour anymore, his long-loved girlfriend ends up breaking off their relationship. While being realistic in describing the emotional and physical aspects of human relationships, the work is at the same time uncompromising in its portrayal of life.

_ **Finding meaning in decadence**
If you were to describe LOAFING AROUND, you might not find it to be the most elegantly written piece of literature. If you were a censor, you might even be inclined to call the book "indecent" with respect to the book's portrayal of sex:

"The woman aggressively pulls the man deep into the darkness of her vagina, not intending to release until they both are fully satiated in the carnal pleasures of the flesh."

Hardly an emotional heart-to-heart conversation; rather, it is just the interaction of two people having fun in order to pass the time.

People tend to associate the adjective "decadent" to Shi Kang's work. You might even spiral down in decadence after reading his books. This is an exaggeration of course, but Shi Kang dismisses this view as too superficial. According to Shi Kang, his work has its roots in reality. It is an earnest call for people to be vigilant, open-minded, unbiased and hard-working. As for him, he strives to maintain an energetic attitude towards life in general in order to write honestly. Even amid the negativity found in

LOAFING AROUND, the book does have a positive message in the end: should you one day, realise the smallness and trifling worth of your existence in this vast world, then no matter the kind of effort that you will exert, it will be the more arduous, enduring and longer-lasting than anyone who is obsessed with worthless and superficial pedantries. In other words, the decadence in the book serves as a wake-up call to readers: it asks them to find their inner strength for overcoming their limits.

_ Stuck in revision limbo

Shi Kang was only twenty-seven after finishing LOAFING AROUND. His friends tended to describe him as a quintessential "angry youth." He would for example be quick to disagree with you, and would hold baseless, yet long tirades about almost everything. His literary work at the time was almost like a mirror to his fiery personality. When the Writers Publishing House published the first edition of LOAFING AROUND, Shi Kang derisively called this the "edited edition." His friend Yang Kui, who was the managing editor at the time, exerted his utmost to win approval for publication. When the book finally hit the bookstores, three years had passed.

The first one to budge was Shi Kang. He finally got tired of waiting, and ceased his resistance against the edits to his manuscript. Moreover, he decided to revise the work together with Yang Kui. Shi Kang was, in his own words, extremely unwilling, but he could only begrudgingly accept the suggestions of his managing editor in order to give the book more leeway with the approval process. At the time, he consoled himself with the observation that a book without readers is but a half-finished product in his own hands. The book would lose its meaning if he were its only reader. Therefore, Shi Kang sat next to Yang Kui at his editing desk, and started the painful process of deleting and reworking his manuscript, one page at a time. His feeling at the time could be likened to sitting on a pincushion, while his manuscript was sent to the butcher shop.

The "edited" edition was finally released; however, Shi Kang was all but satisfied with the end result. He could not comprehend the edits and had voiced his complaints to Yang Kui on numerous occasions. From his perspective, the changes had either changed or warped the original intent of the story. Nevertheless, no matter how you look at it, the facts show that the edited edition paved the road to success for Shi Kang's writing career. The edits and suggestions—inexplicable as they may seem at the time—did ultimately result in the enormous sales number of LOAFING AROUND.

Shi Kang admits that, from a certain perspective, the edits may have led to a better result than what could be expected for the original manuscript. Some readers might even prefer the edited version to the original. It is even likely that other readers would not even see the difference between the two versions. Nevertheless, he, as the creator of the book, would still prefer to let the audience read his original version when given the choice. Therefore when the opportunity came to publish LOAFING AROUND in its original version in 2005, Shi Kang gratefully accepted.

_ Beating around the bush

In China, even someone as Shi Kang, who can be direct with his words, needs to be careful in his literary work. The reason is simple: a lot of things cannot be publicly talked about in China. Whether you have the right to voice your opinion, or even the right to choose an opinion, depends on your identity in the end. Some people are not able to speak out, simply because they have the wrong identity. Other people, who do possess the right to speak, either lack the authority or are completely unqualified to do so. Even if they speak, it would lack anything meaningful.

Language is arguably invented for the purpose of human communication. Shi Kang argues that the Chinese people are part of the human race as much as anyone else. According to him, rules came into being together with the invention of language. These same rules have made man anxious and afraid of talking freely. In China, speaking one wrong word can lead to capital punishment. When speaking promotes anxiety, anxiety will only lead to hesitation. This very hesitation influences the way Chinese people think; furthermore, it degrades and slows down their thinking in the process. Without ever realising it, the Chinese people have been living all the time in an environment filled with anxiety, fear and hopelessness.

Shi Kang has surrendered himself to the thought that, in this situation, neither his own understanding nor his own desires matter anymore. He can only make peace with the fact that anyone can project their own interpretation and values on his work, whereas his own interpretation is but one amid many others. Although unwilling, he can only solemnly accept this fact.

_ The troubled existence of a man of letters

According to Shi Kang, working for the government has the best benefits for a writer in China. This is something that has held true for the China in the present as in the past. The responsibilities and tasks include writing policy documents and describing various official guidelines. In other words, this means writing only the things government officials like to hear—in exchange for stable wages. There are certainly some writers that have tried to break with this tradition of "professional flattery." However, when they tried to be more honest in their work, it only resulted in the ire and sanction of the government. In order to shut their mouth, the government subsequently sentences and detains them in prison in order to harass the writer and his family. The risks associated with being a writer is, simply put, much greater than being a politician in present day China.

Looking back, there are some general trends we can see in history. Around the turn of the 20th century, China had a short surge of independent thinkers. Back then, the nation was experimenting with early-capitalism, but all these thinkers disappeared after the establishment of the People's Republic of China. After the economic reforms of Deng Xiaoping, independent writers started to appear again. However, when compared to their forebears, their voices did not have the same reach nor where the messages as powerful. The main problem lies with the fact that they do not have creative freedom over their own work, for the right to censor their work ultimately lies in the hands of the government.

The majority of the writers and screenwriters of today's China are independent thinkers. However, they only have limited ways to express themselves, let alone have the manoeuvring space to speak honestly in public. There are many kinds of truths in general in a society that encompasses many groups and professions, but China has one unwritten rule. It states that the public does not need to see the negative aspects of society. This is why only positive—not negative—news and messages appear in Chinese media. The Chinese literary world is also subjected to this rule, as mentioned earlier (see Chapter 1 - Ran Yunfei). This might be part of some undefined strategy, but Shi Kang sarcastically remarks that the government is actually doing this for the sake of the people. The government believes that the Chinese people need hope; therefore, there is no need for the people to look at the negative aspects of life. They only need to look at its positive aspects.

When the situation is dire, then there is an even greater need for writers to address things that truly matter. The burden for writers in China is heavier than one might imagine. Not only do they need to work conscientiously, they also need to play by the rules before being able to write. Of course, in order to actually make a career out of writing, their work still need to manage to attract the reader's interest. Trying to fulfil all these conditions is almost an impossible proposition. Nevertheless, this is the reality facing all Chinese writers. The bit of creative freedom they might find in contemporary society can be taken away in the blink of an eye. "Why?" you might ask. The answer is simple:

"Because authors are not the ones holding power, how could they even decide what they can write about?"

/ CHAPTER 2
EXILED AUTHORS

/ MA JIAN

_ Abandoning everything in wanderlust

The first time I met Ma Jian was in Cologne. Ma Jian is famous for his literary works as well as his artwork. In the early 1970s, he joined the "Mist Poets." This artist collective, which existed from the mid-1960s until the late 1970s, was created during the Cultural Revolution in order to resist the strict official control on the creative arts. Many poets and artists regularly held meetings at Ma Jian's single-story house at Nanxiao Lane no. 53 in the Dongzhimen district of Beijing. He counts Gao Xingjian as one of his friends—the first Chinese recipient of the Nobel Prize in Literature.

Ma Jian (1953) was born in Qingdao, Shandong province. He worked as a journalist for the "International Department of the All China Federation of Trade Unions" in Beijing. He quit his job after he was detained for organising—or what is deemed to be—extremist art exhibitions. In his essay "Wandering through China," he would write the following:

"Winter 1983, I was released from the police station. The police officer on duty said 'If you do not straighten out soon, it won't be long before you disappear from the face of the earth.'"

With his newfound freedom, Ma Jian had decided to travel around China. Ma Jian prepared a coupon for a water canister and with a copy of Walt Whitman's "Leaves of Grass" in hand; he left Beijing for a life on the road. He was headed for Tibet as he left the red painted walls of Beijing behind.

Tibet at the time was often romanticised as a picturesque utopia for artists desiring to escape the constraints of an urban lifestyle. Ma Jian most likely shared the same ideals as his contemporaries. One problem that Ma Jian immediately had to face was the fact that he needed official papers for travelling around. Leaving your residency would actually violate the household registry laws. To solve this problem, Ma Jian stole a couple of recommendation letters from his work unit. However, this was only the start of his problems. Ma Jian would be living constantly on the edge: not only did Ma Jian need to find ways to keep himself alive as a wandering tramp, but he also needed to escape the gaze of vigilant citizens and policemen who were on the lookout for stragglers such as Ma Jian. What astonished Ma Jian during this period was the degree of successful indoctrination of the local population at the hands of the communist party. In the several thousand miles he had travelled, locals had reported Ma Jian to the police at least seven times, even forcing him to run for his life on several occasions.

_ The storm of STICK OUT YOUR TONGUE

After his vagabond lifestyle came to an end, Ma Jian decided to write down his experiences of Tibet in the novel STICK OUT YOUR TONGUE. In this book, Ma Jian described the Tibetan culture, lifestyle, customs and religious mythology. He also detailed the process of a "sky burial." After finishing his book, Ma Jian let his friend Gao Xingjian read it. Gao Xingjian praised Ma Jian for his work and recommended the book to Liu Xinwu—the newly appointed editor-in-chief at *People Literature*. Liu Xinwu wanted to leave a big impact at the start of his new career. He also wanted to have a venue for the often criticised and suppressed genre of the "New Realist Literature"; therefore, Ma Jian's manuscript came at a convenient time. Liu Xinwu soon decided to publish the whole novel in a double issue of *People Literature* in 1987. However, things changed for the worse after that.

The story immediately turned into a political problem as soon as it saw publication. In the recollections of Gao Xingjian, he noted that He Jingzhi—the chief officer of the Central Propaganda Department—ordered Liu Xinwu to be relieved from his duties and to undergo official investigation. The department issued a document ordering an immediate stop on the sale of all remaining copies in circulation. These were to be confiscated for destruction. This was also the start of a public smear campaign directed at STICK OUT YOUR TONGUE.

The book was banned for the following reason: "the publication aimed to destroy the ethnic band between the Chinese and Tibet, it is a fabrication purely made for stirring up trouble." Because Liu Xinwu carried full responsibility, he prevented Gao Xingjian from being dragged into this affair. Liu Xinwu's career in the publication world subsequently came to an end. Ma Jian had already moved to Hong Kong, but the incident had significant repercussions for his career in China as his name became a blacklisted word. He may still exist as a citizen, but the state had erased his existence as a writer. From that moment on, he could never make any kind of public appearance in China anymore.

The disappearance of Ma Jian has already continued for more almost two decades. For most people it is almost as if Ma Jian has never existed before. Even till the day of today, Ma Jian needs to use a pseudonym for the occasional publication in order to escape censorship. As unfortunate as it may be, Chinese readers live in a vacuum when it concerns the writer Ma Jian.

_ Farewell my prison society

Ma Jian has lived in Hong Kong and Germany, before settling down in London—his current place of residence. Ma Jian had already found himself wanting to escape from the Chinese "prison society" during the repressive 1970s. However, when Ma Jian finally moved to Hong Kong, which was still under British colonial-rule, he swore to himself that he would not move further away from China. He knew too many authors who have given up on writing as soon as they went overseas. His resolve wavered when Ma Jian was given the opportunity to work as a Chinese lecturer at the Ruhr University Bochum. However, his worst fears came true as Ma Jian realised that he was neglecting his writing after only working for a year at the university. In order to fully immerse himself in writing again, Ma Jian soon quit his teaching job in Germany and moved to England. Soon after his relocation, a publishing house had contracted him as a writer.

Ma Jian met and married Flora Dew after moving to England. This marked the beginning of a fruitful collaboration between Ma Jian and Flora Dew, as Dew studied Chinese contemporary literature at the London University School of Oriental and African Studies and was a very proficient translator of Chinese literature. Dew's translations opened Ma Jian's body of work to the English-speaking public. Ma Jian's fame spread across the globe and his list of prizes and achievements also grew to sizable proportions.

In 2002, Ma Jian wrote about his experiences as a vagabond in the novel RED DUST. This book went on to win the "Thomas Cook Travel Book Award." In 2005, the French monthly literary journal *Lire* awarded Ma Jian a place in their list of "top 50 recommended authors" as their only Chinese entry. In 2009, the book BEIJING COMA won the "Athens Prize for Literature for Greek and Foreign Fiction"—Ma Jian was the first Chinese author to ever win this prize. In the same year, the book had the honour of winning the "Freedom of expression Award" of the London-based publication *Index on Censorship*. Being translated in over thirty languages, Ma Jian's popularity and fame grew on an international level. However, the Chinese versions of his books mainly see publication in Hong Kong or Taiwan.

_Publishing means compromising

Although his work is available all over the world, Ma Jian has always harboured the silent hope to publish his work in China. However, getting access to the publishing market in China is, in the words of Ma Jian, "akin to putting your foot between a quickly closing door; you can only work towards opening a small gap in order to slowly wedge your way inside." Whenever Ma Jian returns to China, he is in constant contact with potential publishers. Ma Jian is even willing to use a pseudonym for his publications in China. Nevertheless, a publication in China often needs heavy editing for an official release. Ma Jian has already accepted this fact; however, he will refrain out of principle from recommending the China-editions of his work. Someday, he might be able to publish his work in China uncensored—and under his own name—but the day when this wish comes to fruition is unfortunately still far in the future.

As an example, take Ma Jian's THE NOODLE MAKER: a scene in the book takes place on the early morning of June fourth—the day of the Tiananmen Square incident; however, in the China-edition, the date is changed to June fifth. The original cover of the book also had several political slogans pasted on the back, but this was removed too. Ma Jian discovered to his horror that, in spite of switching publishers and editors, they all would suggest nearly-identical edits to his manuscript. The edits would sometimes change his book to the point where he could not even recognise his own work anymore. The fact that the book could be released at all can be considered a small miracle in China, but the book remains a compromise to Ma Jian.

Ma Jian already has made peace with the truth that you need to pay a prize when you want to publish in China. Initially, he felt repulsed at the mere thought of changing his work; therefore, he would not allow any kind of edit to his manuscript. Later, he also found out that publishers often have no choice in the matter (as discussed in Chapter 1 - Ye Fu). After understanding the circumstances of the publishers, he reconsidered his stance.

The reason why Ma Jian wants to publish in China is for his work to have some kind of influence on the country and the Chinese people. Weighing in on this fact, Ma Jian finally allowed cuts to his work. He simply found solace in the following fact:

"The edits will allow the publication to succeed [commercially], and it will pave the path for future publications. This means having another shot of publishing a more influential work that is even wider in scope."

THE NOODLE PULLER was finally released by Tianjin Ancient Books House in 2002. This allowed RED DUST to be republished as WANDERING CHINA by New Century Publishing House in 2003.

_BEIJING COMA

One of Ma Jian's most thought-provoking work is BEIJING COMA. Also set during the Tiananmen Square incident, the Chinese-version was released in 2009 on the eve of the twentieth anniversary of the protests. Published by Mirror Books (Hong Kong), the novels contains the recollections of Ma Jian of the Tiananmen Square protest. Ma Jian describes every major events starting from the student unrest of 1986-87 until the fated day of June fourth, 1989.

At the time of the protests, Ma Jian was still in Hong Kong. Upon hearing of the situation in China, he booked the next flight to Beijing and stayed at Tiananmen Square as an onlooker until May 28th, 1989 when his brother suffered a fall at home that left him comatose. While Ma Jian was sitting beside his brother at the hospital bed, he continued following the events on television. When the police crackdown ensued, Ma Jian resolved right there and then to engrave this piece of history in book form. Resolutely he thought to himself the following words

"The communist party may maim and harm the flesh, but neither the party—nor anyone else—can ever exterminate the spirit of man and its collective memory."

In BEIJING COMA, a student falls in a coma after being shot at Tiananmen Square.

Years later, the student finally awakens and finds himself surrounded by apathetic and lethargic people. The student realises that while he was sleeping, the ravages of time have washed the people of their painful memories. They are awake, yet comatose at the same time. He who was unconscious all this time still remembers the painful past as if it happened yesterday. His awakening is like a second death, except he is the one now who has to witness the decay of a whole society that is turning its people into a mass of desensitised beings.

Ma Jian has once state that the book has no chance of finding publication in China. This might sound like an exaggeration, but he is simply being realistic about the situation. As discussed earlier in this book, the merest mention of the Tiananmen-incident will automatically cause censors to ban the work in question. As BEIJING COMA is almost a scathing critique of post-1989 China, it is extremely unlikely that a Chinese publisher will be willing to consider BEIJING COMA for domestic publication.

_Authors-in-exile and banished literature

Many people tend to call Ma Jian an author-in-exile or an exiled author. Some even consider his work to be part of the "banished literature"-genre.

Coincidentally, Ma Jian has once organised a lecture on "Chinese banished literature" at London University. He defined exiled literature as works composed in a situation where the author was forced to leave the country. He argued that in the several thousand years of Chinese history, there has never been a period with true creative freedom. Numerous poets have kept silent due to the political climate of their times. The few people who are willing to express their views only do this in indirect ways. Chinese authors have always hid behind a veil of pseudonyms and metaphors, always refraining from stating anything too direct. This is akin to living in mental banishment. Now, this has become the status quo of Chinese literature, if not the *esprit de corps* of Chinese writers.

When the state would banish an author in the past, it would send said author to a secluded place within China. Although banished authors would need to refrain from appearing in the public for a while, they would still be able to keep living among people with the same language and common culture. However, the party will now exile authors to another country. With one single measure, the state has effectively broken off contact between the author and his or her creative environment. The goal of the Chinese state is to create a hollowed-out author incapable of producing any significant work, let alone resist the sovereignty of the party.

Ma Jian can be considered to be very lucky in this regard. Not only did he not abandon his writing, he has also found a place for himself in international literary. However, there are many more exiled authors who are in less fortunate positions. Exiled authors suddenly need to cope with language barriers in their work and daily lives after being forced out of their country. Unfamiliarity with a new local culture also creates tremendous solitude on a psychological level. Authors need to be brave under such circumstances, but what they also need to do is prevail over their current situation. Nevertheless, reality is often cruel.

Many people cannot endure this kind of situation for a long period of time. Before long, they will abandon their writing, and eventually become lost souls without a place to return home to.

_ To return or not to return to China?

Difficulties abroad have left many exiled authors longing to return home. This is ultimately unfeasible in the long run as these authors often cannot return without suffering from political persecution. Should they return home, then it is likely that they will either attract all kinds of unwanted attention or they will suddenly be spirited away. Ma Jian argues the following:

"You can still be a Chinese author with your own style, disposition and beliefs even when you are abroad; after all, if authors suddenly lose these things after being exiled, then it would not make any difference whether they return to China or not."

The problem facing many exiled authors is that they do not manage to adapt to their new surroundings and be able to grasp its cultural sensibilities. If you also consider for a fact that most of these authors have lost all contact with their home country, it would effectively mean that they are trapped between cultures. What Ma Jian is trying to argue, is that the key to deciding one's fate ultimately lies in one's own hand. You can continue to write about the truths of life as long as you remain abroad; if not, you can only return to an authoritarian state where you will lose all your freedom.

Ma Jian, on his part, has also encountered some difficulty when returning to China. When Ma Jian returned to China in 1994, the border patrol officer at Xi'an Airport detained Ma Jian for one whole night. While he was released the following morning, Ma Jian found out that the police continued to follow him around. The Beijing police chief even invited Ma Jian to drink tea at the police station in order to persuade him not to meet with social activists. Ma Jian has once bemusedly stated that he was an exiled author in name only. During an interview in 2008, Ma Jian noted that he could probably return to China because he has never participated in any kind of social movement. Whenever he returns to China, he neither interacts with too many people, nor will he join any kind of public event, nor will he meet with any sensitive people—he will simply follow the rules. As long as you are willing to cooperate and not go to any extreme ends to prove a point, you will be fine—or so he thought.

The Chinese government finally barred Ma Jian from entering the country in 2011. Although Ma Jian could never find out the reason for his banishment, but from that moment on, Ma Jian became an exiled author both in name and in reality.

_ State-employed authors

Ma Jian actively follows the developments in the Chinese literature world. He is especially critical of the Chinese Writers' Association. He compares the association to the imperial civil examination system of feudal China, where writers use their penmanship to eke out a living as a government official. It is a fact that state-employed authors can enjoy monthly stipends and living arrangements from their government, but their housing and allowance can also be taken away at any moment. Ma Jian argues that this is one the main reason why no famous state-employed author has criticised China and its political system for the past decade. Critical thought has been slowly disappearing under the hegemony of the Communist Party of China.

In today's China, it is entirely possible to risk criminal prosecution just for posting the wrong things on the Internet. That is why state-employed authors never pry too deeply into political topics. Instead, they let a few independent authors explore the boundaries of the Chinese censorship system. Their attitude towards censorship is also apathetic:

"Should you go too far and burn your fingers on censorship, then that is only to be expected; however, should you live to see another day, then you were just lucky this time around."

The fact that state-employed authors systemically avoid anything overtly political is the very mind-set that allows the state to do as it pleases.

Ma Jian is of the opinion that Chinese authors have to worry about two cardinal principles: one is political anxiety, the other is employment anxiety. The former means that the writer has to worry about the things he writes about. As long as their work is fictional and they stay clear from social issues and reality in general, the author-in-question will be fine.

Next to that is the problem of employment anxiety. This means that the author needs to factor in the marketability of his work and how many copies his work will sell in order to make money. As a consequence, authors will try to hold on to their fame for as long as possible when they become successful. The literary merit of their work will only be of secondary concern. Defending the interests of the people; coming into conflict with the state; or presenting a clear viewpoint on political or social problems will be left to more noble authors. The state-employed authors will slowly become desensitised and end up losing their sense of social responsibility. They will only follow the party's guidelines, say the things that are expected of them, and keep their mouths shut when they are told to.

Ma Jian often hears the following words from authors in China, such as:

"You can say whatever you want without repercussions, how could we possibly do that?"

Or:

"How do you expect us to free ourselves? Do you want us to live in poverty? You simply cannot mess with the party!"

"It is as if a knife is constantly held against your throat and they can cut you anytime they like to, would you like to try for yourself?"

"I need to raise a family, should something happen to me, what should they do then?" And:

"I have already given up, people are just like that. Why trouble yourself when you might as well not?"

These words captures the desperation and hopelessness of authors in China. The censors simply control all aspects of the media by making sure that there are no free and counterrevolutionary discourses. Some authors have even accepted their fates and will not question the established order any longer. Television presenters, editors and inexperienced journalists or sometimes even the head of a printing factory often make the mistake of calling the wrath of the censors upon themselves, but state-employed authors never make the mistake of defying the political establishment. From time to time, some news or information might manage to dodge censorship, but the censors will eventually find out sooner or later. The ensuing punishment and investigation will unequivocally be severe.

The only thing that state-employed authors can do is to keep their mouths shut. Ever slowly their minds enter into a dormant state; their literary work will similarly be buried under ground in order to avoid political confrontation. Authors only have three possible options in China:

1 Either remain silent;
2 or go to prison;
3 if not choose death.

Faced with these options, anyone would choose to remain silent.

_ You are just an author, stop meddling with politics!
Ma Jian is of the opinion that authors bear a certain burden:

"Literature and politics are inseparable from each other. You can have as many authors as there are stars in the galaxy, but all authors should possess a certain concern for society. Whenever politics enter the fray of the literary world, then authors should also concern themselves with politics in response. They should continue to do so, until the day when politicians stop concerning themselves with literature."

Numerous people, from police to friends, have tried to "warn" Ma Jian. He would often hear pleas such as "you are an author; please do not involve yourself with politics." Nevertheless, Ma Jian sees this differently. He argues that each person has become involved with politics from the moment they are born in an authoritarian country. An authoritarian government will abuse the law in order to control the very minds of the people. This is precisely the reason why people of the literary profession should stand up to the challenge and take up the burden of responsibility on their shoulders.

All that Ma Jian asks is that authors show their social responsibility towards society. The various social and historical issues described in Ma Jian's work—"Tiananmen-incident," "Cultural Revolution," "one child-policy" and so on—echo this very stance. Ma Jian writes about these issues in order to leave them behind for prosperity's sake. By reading Ma Jian's work, you will come into contact with the historical truths of the past.

Ma Jian feels a deep and loyal sense of responsibility to his occupation as writer. He firmly believes that an author's profession is something that is chosen by someone's own will:

"If you have made that choice, then you should shoulder the burden of responsibility in order to properly face society and reflect upon its problems; it is time for the lethargic authors in China to wake up from their slumber and heed their true calling!"

/ BEI LING

_Exile versus prison

Bei Ling (1959) is an author-in-exile, poet, essayist, literature editor and publisher. Born as Huang Beiling in Shanghai, his family moved to Beijing when he was six years old. The beginning of his literary career can be traced back to college when he started the underground poetry magazine *Tendency* in the 1980s before the Chinese government halted its publication. After that, Bei Ling went to the United States in 1989 as a visiting author and resumed publication of *Tendency* as a literary magazine. When Bei Ling returned to China in 1993, he had brought *Tendency* back to China.

In 2000, when *Tendency* hit its thirteenth issue Bei Ling was sentenced to prison for the "illegal" publication of *Tendency*. His younger brother Huang Fang went to the media to report the arrest of his brother. Although his brother was imprisoned for this, the incident could still be brought under international attention thanks to his plea for help. Thereafter, the State Department of the United States, five Nobel laureates and Susan Sontag—noted writer, influential critic and political activist—all signed a letter of petition to Jiang Zemin—the then incumbent president of China. The content of the letter petitioned that arresting someone on the basis of a literary publication violates international standards. Feeling the pressure, the Chinese government finally decided to give two choices to Bei Ling: 1 go to prison or 2 be an envoy of China (which was a euphemism for being exiled). Thinking over his options, Bei Ling chose the latter option.

On the morning of his departure, Bei Ling was awakened by the police. He brushed his teeth, washed his face and shaved his moustache before he departed from prison grounds. While he sat in the police car, he casted one last glance at the skies of Beijing. He soon arrived at his parent's home on the grounds of Beihang University and bid his last farewells to his family. With one suitcase in hand—something that his family packed overnight—Bei Ling went to the Beijing International Airport with police escorts sending him off on a flight to San Francisco. Bei Ling realised on that very moment that the chances for him to ever return to his home country would be very slim.

Nowadays, Bei Ling tends to stay six months in Taiwan and spends the other half year travelling in Europe and America. Under this arrangement, he spends at least half a year working in a Chinese-language environment, whereas he will be promoting his work, working as a writer-in-residence or giving lectures for the remainder of the year. Bei Ling, as a Chinese author, has made himself feel welcome almost anywhere in the world, except for his country of birth, China.

_ Taking Tendency back to Beijing

When he turned twenty, Bei Ling one day saw the magazine *Today*—the first underground literary journal since the establishment of the People's Republic of China. Bei Ling read about the underground poetry scene and eventually met the founders of the magazine, the notable poets Mang Ke and Bei Dao. Soon enough, Mang Ke invited Bei Ling to attend the literary discussion groups of *Today*, providing Bei Ling with the incredible opportunity to meet with pioneers of contemporary Chinese literature. Through these meetings, Bei Ling would transform from a passive reader into a full-fledged author.

At the time of the Tiananmen-incident, Bei Ling was in the United States. An incident prompted him to prolong his visit in the States, but his good friend Liu Xiaobo—2010 Nobel Peace Prize laureate—was present at the protests. Soon after the incident, state media published an article titled "Arresting the Conspirator Liu Xiaobo." The article also pointed Bei Ling as one of the main culprits behind the protest. Bei Ling's Chinese passport expired while he was abroad, whereas various factors prevented him from renewing his passport. He could finally return in 1993 after he managed to renew his Chinese passport. On his way back to Beijing, he had brought plans to resume the publication of *Tendency*.

As *Tendency* had its roots as an underground magazine, it was almost a given that it would attract the immediate attention of the Chinese state. When the magazine resumed publication overseas, the Chinese government considered exiled dissidents as the main culprits behind the publication. The fact that Bei Ling brought the publication back to China was in the eyes of the Chinese government tantamount to provoking social unrest.

Nevertheless, the government only decided to arrest Bei Ling after *Tendency* hit its fated thirteenth issue. Bei Ling does not think that there is any connection with the aforementioned Tiananmen-incident. As a matter of fact, Bei Ling was not even present at the time of the protests, let alone a participant of the movement. The state would not have been able to trial him for counter-revolutionary crimes. "The main reason," Bei Ling surmises, "has to do with the fact that the underground magazine had simply become too influential to be ignored." Underground magazines are evidently illegal, but what added fuel to the flames and set the situation ablaze was the fact that the printing, advertising, and sale were all done in Beijing. Before the thirteenth issue, Bei Ling had his magazine printed in Hong Kong, but the overhead costs were becoming too steep. When Bei Ling decided to publish his magazine in the very political heart of China, he had in fact painted a big target on his publication. The content of the magazine was another factor that prompted government crackdown.

The sixth issue, for example, contained "The Album of Banished Writings," whereas the ninth issue had "The Album of Contemporary Underground Writings." Furthermore, each issue had a "Compendium of Unofficial Literature of the People's Republic of China" and the "Memorandum of Chinese Authors and Artists." As you can probably see, each part of the publication contains extremely delicate content. It was only a matter of time before the communist party had to stop the publication.

The state saw fit to unleash the full might of the police force to stop Bei Ling's "intellectual poison." The police went through the full repertoire of confiscation, intimidation, imprisonment, foreclosure of the printing factory, and issuing heavy fines. This was all done in order to ensure a stop to one simple publication.

Bei Ling does not plan to let *Tendency* vanish without a trace. He has plans to restart the publication as an international journal for literature, thought and art. Not only will *Tendency* be updated for the 21st century, it will continue to carry on the spirit of its original publication.

_ An unknown author

Bei Ling has remained relatively obscure in China. His only official publication there is TODAY AND TOMORROW, a poem collection that was released through Lijiang publishing in 1988. Bei Ling opted to release his next poem collection THEME AND VARIATIONS in Taiwan in 1994. Bei Ling's works are only published in Hong Kong and Taiwan now; none of his works have seen official publication in China since his TODAY AND TOMORROW. The censors would definitely try to prevent a potential publication from happening, but it is also because Bei Ling does not have any desire to publish in China. Even if he had the chance to publish his work, it is more than certain that he would need to delete or edit huge portions of the content. Bei Ling would simply be unable to accept such modifications to his work. Of course, Bei Ling does harbour the deep wish to publish his work in China some day in the future; however, this is only on the condition that any kind of edit needs to have the express approval of Bei Ling. Should the publisher fail this condition, then Bei Ling would rather remain an unknown existence in China. After his arrest in 2000, Bei Ling has essentially disappeared from public view in China. This does not mean that the Chinese government has let Bei Ling out of its sights. His name is blacklisted and even his participation in overseas activities remains under "home surveillance."

When China was the guest-of-honour country at the Frankfurt Book Fair in 2009, the German organisers initially invited Bei Ling to take part in a discussion panel. However, when Chinese state officials received notice of the invitation, they immediately demanded that the Frankfurt Book Fair retract the invitation of Bei Ling. Although the organisers complied with the request of the Chinese government, Bei

Ling still decided to travel to Frankfurt with his friend Dai Qing—famed journalist and environmental activist—to participate as spectators.

This incident did not go unnoticed by the German media. The Germans criticised the Frankfurt Book Fair for submitting to political pressure from China. Finally on the eve before the official opening, the organisers released an open letter. In this letter, the Frankfurt Book Fair organisation publicly stated that it has received notice of the arrival of Bei Ling and Dai Qing. Not only did the organisers renew their invitation, but they also expressed their wish for Bei Ling and Dai Qing to attend the opening ceremony.

On the day of the opening ceremony the organisers invited Bei Ling and Dai Qing on stage to close the ceremony. However, the moment when Dai Qing took the stage, the official delegation from China suddenly decided to leave the stage in protest. After they left the stage, the Chinese party gave notice that they would withdraw from the book fair entirely. The Frankfurt Book Fair organisers immediately stopped the opening ceremony after this incident and offered their sincere apology to the Chinese delegation. The Chinese delegation party responded that Bei Ling and Dai Qing are not representatives of China, nor are their work representative of Chinese literature. They are only dissidents.

Bei Ling recalled that the *Global Times* had written that Mo Yan—the delegation leader and 2012 Nobel laureate of Literature—had stated that "[Mo Yan] will immediately leave the room if Bei Ling is going to participate in the discussion panel." In the article, Mo Yan claims that Bei Ling is an unknown author in China; therefore, he sees no need to engage in a literary discussion with Bei Ling. When Bei Ling asked Mo Yan on a later occasion to clarify this interview, Mo Yan refuted the claims. He claimed that he had never accepted an interview from the *Global Times*; instead, the reporter projected those words on his public image. However, Mo Yan cannot publicly reject these claims, because he is a state-employed author.

_ The troubles of banishment

Bei Ling has his own interpretation of a life in exile. As authors and intellectuals have fled China in the wake of the Tiananmen-incident, they developed a new kind of Chinese literature, namely that of the "banished literature"-genre. His interpretation includes authors who are residing in China, yet who can only publish in underground or overseas publications. Bei Ling argues that the reflections and memoirs of authors-in-exile are shaped through the notions of nation, ethnicity and personal histories. The accumulated efforts of exiled authors, both overseas as well as domestically, have deepened and brought new horizons to Chinese literature.

Nevertheless, it is almost a guarantee that exiled authors stumble upon many problems after they leave their home country. Bei Ling shares the same sentiment as

Ma Jian, as he points out that the main cause of this phenomenon lies with the forceful changes in the language and cultural environment. He notes that exiled authors will slowly stop writing unless their work can be quickly translated in other languages. This is the reason why the Chinese authors-in-exile have not become a united or influential collective. Outstanding works of literature produced by this group can at most be counted on one hand.

Bei Ling acknowledges that he also suffers from the faults he has mentioned. He considers himself more of a production worker of literature nowadays, while his writing is but a mere shell of his work in China. After he had left China, Bei Ling realised that his state of mind, creativity and inspiration have dulled over time, whereas he has stopped writing poetry. In order to put a halt to this development, Bei Ling has opted to stay at least six months a year in Taiwan for the purpose of remaining in a Chinese language-environment.

Bei Ling has once said the following: "My home is no longer China; my home is the Chinese language." These melancholic words reflect the fact that Bei Ling has found his refuge in the Chinese language; it is a source of strength. English is useful as a tool for daily communication; however, Chinese is what Bei Ling uses to ply his art, for language is arguably the soul of an author.

_ The long road home

Among exiled authors, some have chosen to leave by their own will and to build a new life overseas. Others like Bei Ling were literally chased out of their country. To them, the notion of ever returning to China has become something like a faraway dream. While increasingly more exiled authors have found opportunity to return home and see their loved ones, Bei Ling is still barred from entering China. Although he has no desire to lose his dignity and self-worth, Bei Ling merely wants to visit China, even if it is only for a short while, out of a desire to see his family. His most cherished wish is to see his parents.

As holiday seasons pass by each year, Bei Ling becomes even more overwhelmed by pangs of homesickness. Especially the Lunar Festival is hard for Bei Ling as this is traditionally celebrated with the family. He just wants to tell the Chinese government that during this time of the year, everyone will temporarily cease their indifferences—regardless of their affiliation or political orientation—and return home in order to have a traditional New Year's dinner. This desire has followed Bei Ling for many years, yet it remains unfulfilled in spite of his efforts.

In 2009, after the end of the Frankfurt Book Fair, Bei Ling booked a flight from Frankfurt to Taipei. He would transfer once in Beijing. When Bei Ling handed over his passport and boarding pass to the border inspection, the officer frowned when he entered Bei Ling's name in his terminal. While he kept his eyes glued on the monitor, his hand grabbed the nearby telephone. Bei Ling's heart sank when he heard the officer speak the following words:

"There is a small situation over here, please call some people over."

Bei Ling saw the border patrol officer arriving to study his personal information in detail. In the next moment, the officer asked Bei Ling:

"Is your name Huang Beiling?" To which Bei Ling replied:

"Yes. Is there a problem, officer?"

"We just need to confirm your identity. What is your date of birth?"

After Bei Ling returned the answer, the officer asked Bei Ling to come with him in order to "verify" some information. The officer gave no reply when Bei Ling asked whether he was being blacklisted.

Around this time, two police officers wearing mouth masks have joined them. Three people escorted Bei Ling to the "questioning room." The border patrol officer took Bei Ling's passport with him and exited the room.

Thirty minutes later another border patrol officer entered with Bei Ling's passport in his hand. Loudly he declared:

"We have confirmed that you are prohibited from entering the country. You may neither enter Beijing, nor are you allowed to move around before boarding your flight to Taipei. You will be placed under police custody during the remainder of your stay at the Beijing International Airport."

Bei Ling, who was hoping to finally reunite with his parents after a long period of separation, was shocked and could only speak in a trembling voice:

"Don't you know that I'm from Beijing? How could you not understand what Beijing means to me?! My ageing parents live just a couple of miles from here, you'd surely know that! How many people are there on the black list that share the same fate as me? What kind of crime did we violate? Please tell me! For what reason have I been denied entry? Please tell me the reason, why!?"

After waiting for Bei Ling to finish, the police officers glanced at the border patrol officer who only dryly stated:

"I wouldn't know, but you'd probably understand your own situation better than we do."

Afterwards, Bei Ling sat between two police officers at the Terminal 3 waiting hall. One of the police officers was holding his passport and boarding pass, while the other kept his gaze locked on Bei Ling.

While he was waiting for the plane, Bei Ling asked one of the officers whether he knew why Bei Ling has barred from entering china.

"I don't know," answered the officer, "you look very well-mannered."

"It's because I write literature," answered Bei Ling.

After hearing these words from the mouth of Bei Ling, the police officer just merely held his mouth, seemingly unable to find a response to this.

Bei Ling went through the boarding gate holding one suitcase in hand while the two officers escorted him. The police officers only returned his passport and boarding pass when Bei Ling was about to enter the plane. The police officers remained at the boarding gate entrance until the plane had taxied away and departed from the airport. Bei Ling felt his heart ache when the plane finally departed. As he wept, Bei Ling kept wondering the following question: "How he could have become a *persona non grata* in his very own country?"

Bei Ling's flight departed for Taipei, but his luggage was held back in Beijing. He would eventually receive his luggage later in the evening back in Taipei; however, Bei Ling would not be as fortunate the next time.

Bei Ling tried to take the same transfer flight from Frankfurt to Taipei in 2010. As soon as his flight landed on Beijing airport, Bei Ling was surrounded by twenty police officers. They took him to a nondescript building where they detained him for two hours. A police officer announced that Bei Ling was forbidden from transiting from Beijing to Taipei. This order was to be followed to the letter with no exceptions allowed. After this announcement, the police took Bei Ling away in a police car and placed him on the return flight to Frankfurt. Bei Ling had hurt his back during this ordeal, but what hurt even more was the fact that the police also held his luggage back that contained his handwritten memoirs—the manuscript for EXILED.

Compared to a year ago, the Chinese state was prepared for the arrival of Bei Ling. This most likely had to do with the Nobel Peace Prize awarded to the political dissident Liu Xiaobo that year. In order to commemorate this event, Bei Ling had decided to issue a biography of his good friend. The Chinese state would forcefully prevent Bei Ling from entering China in retribution.

_ A Panopticon with Chinese characteristics

Although he cannot return to his country, Bei Ling still has a proper grasp on the domestic situation of China. He argues "that present day authors are facing one of the darkest periods at the moment in Chinese history." Since the new party leadership have taken over the reins of the country, social activists and human rights defenders, such as authors and lawyers, have suffered increased suppression and persecution. A new low has been reached with respect to Internet control, media supervision and public gag orders. Such measures have transformed the Chinese nation into a giant Panopticon. It is turning many independent thinkers and literati into prisoners who have no means to escape.

Bei Ling argues that state-employed authors are lying when they claim that there is no censorship in China. If state-employed authors, for example, start espousing the virtues of democracy and freedom and deviate from official discourse, then they, too, would risk attracting the ire of the party. You will be sent into exile sooner or later when you manage to irritate the party, government or even to become an obstacle to their plans. Being a state-employed author evidently does not serve as an insurance against state persecution.

As our interview came to an end, Bei Ling shared a smile with me. As we parted our ways, he said one final thing to me:

"I am but an old exiled warrior."

/ LIAO YIWU

_ First encounters with the grandmaster

"Bald, glasses and a wig, just like a great sage" that was my first impression of Liao Yiwu. When the Norwegian Nobel Academy decided to award the "Nobel Literature Prize" to Mo Yan in 2012, the German Publishers and Booksellers Association (Börsenverein des Deutschen Buchhandels) awarded the "Peace Prize of the German Book Trade" to the exiled author Liao Yiwu. Who is Liao Yiwu and what has he done to deserve such a prize?

Born in Yanting, Sichuan province, Liao Yiwu (1958) is also known by his pen name Lao Wei. Known as a poet, author-in-exile and historiographer of the lower ranks of society, Liao Yiwu currently resides in Berlin, Germany. Liao Yiwu got his start in literature by frequently publishing in official publications during the 1980s. His award-winning, sometimes avant-garde poetry tends to strike a rebellious tone—this was possible during the 1980s as the political climate was comparatively relaxed. Nevertheless, Liao Yiwu suffered severe criticism during political campaigns, such as the "Anti-Spiritual Pollution Campaign" and "Anti-Bourgeois Liberalisation Campaign," that were aimed at stopping such boisterous poetry.

The harsher the criticism, the more Liao Yiwu would push back. He would redirect his rebellious energy towards starting various underground publications in which he could freely publish his compositions. As these underground magazines were inherently illegal, it goes without saying that these magazines would often suffer censorship and police crackdowns. Liao Yiwu owes his years of experience as an escape artist to these confrontations with the law.

_ Prison time caused by "Massacre"

In spite of his fair share of confrontations with the law, Liao Yiwu was still unwilling to quit writing. From 1986 to 1989 he would publish a series of long-form poetry; however, the real turning point came during the student protests in 1989. In the spring of 1989, street protests had broken out all over the nation. This proved to be an omen for the protests on Tiananmen Square in June 1989. The early protests prompted Liao Yiwu to start writing his poem "Massacre." In this poem, Liao Yiwu had foreseen the violence that would ultimately befall upon the protesters at the hands of the People's Liberation Army. As he did not possess the means to have the poem published on a large scale, Liao Yiwu decided to stand at the Tiananmen Square on the morning of June fourth and to start loudly reciting his poem amid the protesters. Afterwards, he recorded the poem on cassette tape and distributed the tapes across the country.

On begin March 1990, Liao Yiwu started to record the cinematic successor to "Massacre"—the poetry film "Requiem." The film was meant to be a soliloquy for the deceased protesters of Tiananmen Square. However, one month had not even passed in recording before Liao Yiwu and ten other members of his film crew were arrested by the National Security Bureau in Chongqing. Ten other poets and authors at various other locations were also arrested and detained. All of them were people who contributed to "Massacre" in one form or another. One of those people was the spouse of Liao Yiwu who, at the time, was pregnant with his child. In the aftermath of this crackdown, the state charged Liao Yiwu with political crimes, branded him as a counterrevolutionary and sentenced him to four years of prison.

While in prison, he attempted to commit suicide at least four times. It would not be an exaggeration to say that compared to the average citizen or political activist, Liao Yiwu has tempted fate on far too many occasions. Liao Yiwu was finally released forty-three days earlier for "good behaviour" on January 31st, 1994.

_ The arduous life after prison

Released from prison, Liao Yiwu had to endure all kinds of suffering. His wife and child left him, while his friends from the literary circle have all gone into hiding. In the eyes of the public, Liao Yiwu has become somewhat like a sore wound, if not a reminder of a past they would like to forget. Liao Yiwu was a poet, but he had trouble making ends meet after his release from prison—writing had simply become a luxury. Liao Yiwu had a brief stint as a chef and as a wandering tramp. Moreover, he had learnt to play the Chinese flute while in prison. Using his performance skills, he would perform in bars and teahouses in order to eke out a living. Nevertheless, he still strove to keep on writing in spite of his circumstances. However, whenever he would finally find his way back in the publication world, he would often find out that his ventures are destined to be short-lived.

In 1996, Liao Yiwu was dismissed from a magazine publication because the National Security Bureau repeatedly warned the publication against employing Liao Yiwu. In 1997, Liao Yiwu attempted to open a bookstore; however the National Security Bureau promptly dispatched an investigation team to confiscate his wares, forcing Liao Yiwu to abandon his newly-found business. In 1998, after two months of working at the *Chengdu Economic Daily*, the National Security Bureau, once again, gave a warning to the editor-in-chief and the editorial board. The end result was the same: Liao Yiwu found himself living on the streets again. The state pro-actively prevented Liao Yiwu from ever working in the publication industry.

_ Publication-killer

Liao Yiwu has endured the full brunt of state persecution, ranging from the confiscation of his wares to the termination of his employment. These acts of institutionalised harassment all fall within the scope of state censorship. This is what could befall any author who dares to go against the Chinese government. From the moment Liao Yiwu became a poet, he had embroiled himself in censorship. In the beginning of his publication career, he published his long-form poem "The City of Death" in the magazine *People Literature*—one of the first literary magazines to be created in the People's Republic of China. This work soon received (official) resistance and criticism. He created two other long-form poems in 1989—"Yellow city" and "Idol"—that were direct criticisms aimed at Mao Zedong. These two poems caused Liao Yiwu unending trouble in the aftermath of Tiananmen Square.

Moreover, the Central Propaganda Department order the disbandment the magazine *Frontier* that had published one of the poems. Liao Yiwu was simply forbidden from releasing any kind of publication or opinion piece in public.

These matters are but trivial when compared to later events. In 1999, Liao Yiwu had finally an opportunity to publish his works in China. He published two works, namely FALL OF THE HOLY TEMPLE: AN ANTHOLOGY OF UNDERGROUND POEMS FROM THE 1970S (Xinjiang Youth Press) and INTERVIEWS WITH THE MARGINALISED (China Drama Publishing House).

The latter work is a treatise on the underbelly of Chinese society. It contains interviews conducted with murderers, thieves, human traffickers, fortune tellers, fengshui masters, homosexuals, beggars, political dissidents and brothel procurers. The protagonists of the book are essentially people who belong to the "lower caste" of society. After the book saw public release, it became an instant bestseller, becoming an unofficial classic in Chinese New Realism. However, it did not take long before the General Administration of Press and Publication decided that the book is a "reactionary work." Liao Yiwu's efforts to uncover the hidden side of society resulted in a police search of the printing factory. The state even issued police warrants for the publishing house. What is truly shocking is what took place on February 1999. The police took Liao Yiwu into custody on the day when he was supposed to be celebrating his second marriage. He spent the day at the police station as the police conducted an illegal search of the premises.

Despite these setbacks, Liao Yiwu still did not give up on writing. During the spring of 2001, he used his pen name Lao Wei to release the abridged version of INTERVIEWS WITH THE LOWER STRATA OF CHINESE SOCIETY (Changjiang Publishing House). The response of the media was intense: fifty different publications reported and disseminated the book. Dozens of experts and hundreds of readers would meet up at the Beijing *Guo Lin Feng* bookstore to hold heated discussions about the book. One evening an assembly of people met up at the Temple of Enlightenment—one of Beijing's old Buddhist temples. Amid this large gathering, Liao Yiwu started reciting his poem "Massacre." As readers might know by now, such a big and public event in China will immediately provoke a reaction from the state. In the resulting aftermath, the state banned INTERVIEWS WITH THE LOWER STRATA OF CHINESE SOCIETY, issued arrest warrants for the responsible book company and closed down the print factory. The publishing house also received disciplinary actions and remaining books on the streets were all confiscated. From that moment on, Liao Yiwu became known as the "publication-killer." Now, there is no publisher in China anymore that is willing to contract his books.

The Southern Weekend—a progressive news publication in South-China—dedicated a whole issue to Liao Yiwu and his INTERVIEWS WITH THE LOWER STRATA OF CHINESE SOCIETY. The state severely reprimanded the magazine as a result: on April 19th, 2001, the editor-in-chief, vice-editor-in-chief, editorial board and the respective directors of the news and publication groups all needed to hand in their resignation. Liao Yiwu only understood as much as anyone else as he was just a bystander in this affair. He received a telephone call from a friend that worked as an editor in South-China. His friend could only confide the following to him:

"Liao Yiwu; for your own sake, you'd better remain silent for the next decade."

_ Unending harassment

After Liao Yiwu was released from prison, he was under constant surveillance. It did not matter where he went or what he did, state officials just wanted to prevent him from writing again. Initially, they had offered Liao Yiwu a chance to switch to another career track, such as becoming a clothing salesman. After Liao Yiwu rejected all their offers, the state officials decided to change their methods. From that moment on, the state would relentlessly follow Liao Yiwu and unmercifully suppress all of his activities.

Liao Yiwu would eventually write the book TESTIMONIALS following his release from prison. An abridged form of this book would be later released in the west as FOR A SONG AND A HUNDRED SONGS: A POET'S JOURNEY THROUGH A CHINESE PRISON. In this book, Liao Yiwu writes about his experiences in prison and reveals some hidden truths about Chinese prisons. Liao Yiwu's attempts at writing this book have caused him to attract unwanted attention from the state censorship on multiple occasions.

The first incident was after Liao Yiwu had written a composition of over three hundred thousand words after writing non-stop for one year. Liao Yiwu efforts were wasted as the police confiscated his manuscript soon thereafter. This was an enormous setback for Liao Yiwu. Following this incident the police placed Liao Yiwu under house arrest for almost one month. Undeterred, Liao Yiwu mustered his courage once again and wrote another two hundred thousand words on paper within one year. However, this manuscript was also confiscated. Not willing to give up, Liao Yiwu decided for his third attempt to write on computer and store the file on a floppy disk hidden in a safe location. This attempt ultimately proved futile too, as the floppy disk was also confiscated.

Liao Yiwu has once sent a letter to several good friends, in which he describes the following house search on December 18th, 2002:

"The police showed an official subpoena with a search warrant and recorded the entire process. The present officers 'earnestly' made an effort at compiling an inventory of the confiscated items, leaving an extra copy for him behind. They even sent the chief of the police station to act as a witness."

Liao Yiwu would later recall that "this house search was conducted in fairly civil matter, especially compared to house searches in the past." Liao Yiwu already has had some experience with police searches before he was sent to prison; nevertheless, the next "visit" thoroughly shocked Liao Yiwu to the core of his being.

One day, the phone suddenly rang at six in the morning. It was still dark outside, yet the phone kept ringing for five minutes straight without any sign of stopping. When the spouse of Liao Yiwu woke up in order to pick up the phone, she suddenly heard loud bangs on the front door. The sound of the ringing telephone intertwined with the bangs on the door; slowly creating an oppressive and tense atmosphere. When his wife opened the door, three strangers barged into the house. One of those strangers, who appeared to be the leader, sternly announced that they were issuing a subpoena to Liao Yiwu and shouted for him to come down. When Liao Yiwu's wife had hurriedly exited their home, the man phoned for five more men. Eight burly men had started the house search. Their primary objective was Liao Yiwu's computer, although they also carefully searched his bedroom drawer and study room.

The whole ordeal had lasted for three hours by the time the men had finished their search. They left the premises with Liao Yiwu in tow and his computer, which contained a manuscript of several hundred thousands of words. The men placed Liao Yiwu in a police car and drove to the local police station in order to interrogate him.

The investigators questioned Liao Yiwu on his alleged participation in social movements and suspicious activities on the Internet. Liao Yiwu flatly denied all accusations. When the policemen had finished their questions, they released Liao Yiwu in the late afternoon. Before he left, the police told him to stay at home while he waited for their official subpoena. Liao Yiwu immediately went into a nearby Internet cafe and promptly deleted his email in-box and contacts list. After all his experiences with the police, the one thing that Liao Yiwu is still afraid of is the potential harm to his family and friends. Should he neglect to delete all possible leads to them, it is possible that he would have to start worrying about their well-being.

Liao Yiwu finally decided to publish TESTIMONIALS in Germany since he knew that there was no chance of having his book published in China. He primarily conducted his business through e-mail; however, Chinese officials found about his plans through their continued surveillance of his online communication. They probably ordered a house search in order to prevent Liao Yiwu from publishing his book in Germany. Should the book be published, then Liao Yiwu would risk a prison sentence of ten years. This prompted German publishers to fear for his personal safety; thus, they decided to push back the publication date of his book. Liao Yiwu saw two outcomes if he is going to publish his book: either he goes to prison or he leaves the country. Liao Yiwu chose to leave.

_ So long China!
Liao Yiwu would be stopped sixteen times at the border patrol checkpoint. It is almost a given that leaving China will not be an easy feat considering Liao Yiwu's official rap sheet. At some point, the police even warned him that if he tried leaving through Beijing International Airport one more time, he will most likely "disappear" for an indefinite period of time.

Liao Yiwu finally managed to obtain a passport in 2008 against all odds. The National Security Bureau had tried to prevent this from happening on several previous occasions. Liao Yiwu soon received an invitation from the Frankfurt Book Fair in 2009, but he could not attend the event due to his travelling difficulties. A similar situation occurred again for the Cologne Literature Festival in 2010. Liao Yiwu was detained at the airport and questioned for several hours straight. Liao Yiwu finally resorted to petitioning directly to the Chancellor of Germany in order to ask for help. Only after a high level diplomatic talk, where the Chancellor expressed her wish to see Liao Yiwu, did the Chinese state allow Liao Yiwu to briefly leave the country. On September 2010, Liao Yiwu finally managed to attend the International Literature Festival of Berlin—his first visit abroad.

Liao Yiwu soon made plans to visit other countries, but the Chinese state had decided to restrict his movements and place a travelling ban on Liao Yiwu for "national security reasons." During this ordeal Liao Yiwu would constantly think the following to himself:

"I'll definitely escape this country and leave this draconian 'home' behind; [if given the choice] I'd rather be in a world that relies on compassion and reason to differentiate between good and evil; and right and wrong."

Liao Yiwu finally decided to depart for Germany permanently via the Sino-Vietnamese border on June 2011. As soon as he boarded the plane from Hanoi to Germany, Liao Yiwu's exiled lifestyle had begun.

Liao Yiwu currently lives a calm and tranquil life in Germany. Whenever someone asks him whether he wants to return to China, he determinedly answers: "I will not return as long as the Communist Party of China remains in power." Liao Yiwu does feel a desire to visit his ancestral home in Sichuan one day; however there is not much lost love between him and China. Living in China has been like one long nightmare for Liao Yiwu.

Liao Yiwu continues to write in spite of living in a country where he has trouble communicating. However, according to Liao Yiwu, "[he has] seen and heard enough stories to last an entire lifetime." Living in a free country means that Liao Yiwu can fully showcase his creative talent. The time when he was unable to produce or to publish anything is now but a thing of the past. His writing has attracted a legion of loyal readers and won him many awards, while Liao Yiwu has become a frequent guest at various literature festivals. His parents probably would have never imagined that their child, once sentenced to prison for his poetry, would become one of the most popular Chinese authors in the west.

_ The German peace prize debacle

On June 2012, the German Publishers and Booksellers Association of the Federal Republic of Germany announced that they would award Liao Yiwu with the "Peace Prize of the German Book Trade." This was the first time in sixty-two years since the establishment of the peace prize that it would be awarded to a Chinese author. Liao Yiwu won the prize, because he vehemently protests against state oppression and adamantly rejects the totalitarian regime in China. In the "banished literature"-genre, there are few authors who can express their political views in a clean and distinct manner such as Liao Yiwu. There was even one occasion where he brazenly announced that "the imperial state of China will inevitably come to an end." Liao Yiwu was subtly pointing out the parallel between the communist party and the ancient Chinese empires that would always end up robbing people of their rights under the guise of unification.

The Chinese government responded with sharp criticism. A spokesperson for the Chinese Ministry of Foreign Affairs stated during a press conference that "Liao Yiwu was imprisoned for illegal conduct; he is making up stories to win the support and sympathy of the people abroad." The *Global Times*—an official state publication in China—published three critical articles deriding the views of Liao Yiwu as dissident.

These articles also questioned his mental health and argued that his judgement and emotional being must be judged differently from regular people. Liao Yiwu bemusedly considers these personal attacks as a form of publicity: thanks to these articles, his family in China can stay up-to-date with his current movements.

In any case, the German award committee members have a clear stance on this matter: they think that "Liao Yiwu continues to wage an eloquent and fearless battle against political repression and who lends a clear and unmistakable voice to the downtrodden and disenfranchised of his country." The committee also praised him as "an unrelenting advocate of human dignity, freedom and democracy."

_ The worrisome Chinese situation

Liao Yiwu thinks that state-employed authors have no choice but to dance to the tune of the communist party. They would for instance claim that "China, at present, has entered an unparalleled golden era." While it is true that the Chinese economy and culture have made exceptionally progress, there does not appear to be any serious discussion of its censorship problem. Of course, there are some state-employed authors who chose the middle road. These people criticise the current Chinese society, but they will forgo any real opinion on political matters. The middle road decidedly refrains from choosing any side. State-employed authors ultimately do not provide any real resistance against the authoritarian rule of the party, nor will their critiques be as thorough as exiled authors. Liao Yiwu can empathise with the destitute conditions of these authors, but it is not a path he would choose for himself.

The state maintains social stability by giving the people food, housing and a car parked in front of their home. People who live of the government like this slowly become desensitised to the problems in their environment. Instead, they will find themselves unwilling and unable to part with such material comforts. By financing such a lifestyle, the state ensures your allegiance and coerces you into speaking on behalf of the communist party. In order to escape the allure of such material benefits, Liao Yiwu had chosen to escape.

Liao Yiwu had once confessed to his friends that he chose banishment, because he was afraid to go to prison again. He stated that the circumstances in China have turned for the worse these past years as many activists and independent thinkers have disappeared without a trace. Should Liao Yiwu be imprisoned again under the current regime, then it is likely that he would spent the remainder of his life in prison. Liao Yiwu found himself left with no option other than to leave China.

Liao Yiwu considers documenting the hardships of life as his main responsibility now. He argues that as things and events are written down on paper, it becomes something that will last forever as part of mankind's heritage. Only by documenting the truth can you shine a beacon of wisdom for future generations. This provides a basis that allows our children to achieve even greater accomplishments.

/ ZHOU QING

_ From young author to prisoner

Zhou Qing is a documentary maker, an editor, a political critic and an exiled author and is famous for his research into local traditions, folklore, and oral history. Ever since he was exiled in 2008, Zhou Qing has been residing in Berlin, Germany.

Born in the city of Xi'an, Shaanxi province, Zhou Qing was considered to be a writing prodigy as a youth. He released his debut novel when he was eighteen and studied at the "Lu Xun Literary Institute" of the Chinese Writers' Association; furthermore, he nurtured his talent at the "Writers' class" of Northwest University (Xi'an). He had considerable influence as an author, but in 1989, Zhou Qing was sentenced to two years in prison for his participation in the protests at Tiananmen Square, Beijing.

While he was imprisoned, the prison administration added another eight months to his sentence as punishment for an attempted escape. He was charged with "poor behaviour for refusing to accept re-education." From that moment on, the communist party considered Zhou Qing a "dangerous entity." Zhou Qing would suffer torture in prison for his transgressions, but the biggest price he had to pay was the loss of his identity.

_ From fantasy to reality

Although he has faced many troubles in life, Zhou Qing has never forsaken his writing. His work focuses on historical and contemporary problems of China, where his topics can range from "a study on the handwritten memoirs of the Cultural Revolution" to "his experiences as an exiled author in China." Zhou Qing started his writing career as a novelist, but his early work lacked the social awareness that would develop in his later work. The protests in 1989 would help Zhou Qing find his future writing style. Zhou Qing has once said the following words:

"The Chinese social situation reality beats the imagination and creativity of any novelist or dramatist as it's more exaggerated and absurd than what the most creative mind in the nation can think up of. It does not matter what aspect of reality you delve into, you'll definitely find something in China that will scare you to death."

Writing in a social responsible way is not easy to do, but Zhou Qing ardently tries to make a contribution. He has spent two years investigating the food safety problem of

China in exhausting detail and wrote the results of his investigation in the book WHAT KIND OF GOD: A SURVEY OF THE CURRENT SAFETY OF CHINA'S FOOD. Zhou Qing received the "2006 Lettre Ulysses Award for the Art of Reporting" for this book. This book on China's food safety problem became an international bestseller and saw release in 10 different countries, including China.

In order to fully understand China's food safety problem, Zhou Qing travelled across the country to find information for his book. The investigation was in his words "even more dangerous than investigating drug dealers." Food producers of shoddy products, especially those with ties to government officials, all understand the consequences of what such an investigation would entail. They are prepared to kill in order to prevent their secrets from leaking. The intertwined interests of the private sector with state power have led to its only logical result: whoever dares to expose the truth will suffer from severe consequences.

Zhou Qing concludes from his research that bad food products have its root in the general mind-set of the Chinese people. In a country with constantly changing policy guidelines, it is often safer "to speak nonsense than to speak straight." The basis of the Chinese state and its economic development are built upon lies. Lying about history and deluding the people have become the accepted norm rather than the exception. Zhou Qing argues that the people have begun to accept the misguidance of the government without really understanding what this can cause. They only realise the full extent of this problem after they become victims of said lies. "If people who want to continue deluding themselves in spite of knowing the truth," argues Zhou Qing, "then sooner or later, they will be unable to differentiate between fiction and reality."

_ Censorship, surveillance and violence

When his book WHAT KIND OF GOD saw release in 2006, only eight thousand copies were pressed in China before the censors prohibited the publication. Zhou Qing had deleted one-third of the content before release, yet his efforts were in vain. Of course, his experiences with censorship are far from limited to this occasion only.
His imprisonment in 1989 mostly had to do with a petition he wrote for the protesters.

The state considered the petition an "illegal work that used democracy and freedom as a pretext." Following his release from prison, Zhou Qing was placed under strict surveillance for an indefinite period of time. During the state visit of Bill Clinton—then the incumbent president of the United States—the police urged Zhou Qing to stay at home. Afterwards, one of his neighbours told him that many "strange" cars were patrolling the area—surveillance cars from the police! The police forced Zhou Qing to travel to another place during the presidential visit. The police made sure that Zhou Qing would not disappear from their sights. When Zhou Qing went to Hunan province, he would "coincidentally" meet the two policemen from Xi'an that were responsible for monitoring him. The local police had located Zhou Qing using its full manpower and one single photograph. Even outside of Beijing, Zhou Qing would remain under constant surveillance of the police.

Zhou Qing was forbidden from appearing in Chinese media for a significant amount of time. Zhou Qing decided to adopt the name Jing Li as his pen name when he had the opportunity again to reappear in public media. On the one hand, it is regrettable that Zhou Qing cannot use his own name for his publications in China, but on the other hand, Zhou Qing is convinced that authors are identified through the worth of their own work. However, when you take away their right of publication, then it is akin to taking away an author's identity:

"This is institutionalised torture; it is designed to humiliate authors and push them to the brink of oblivion, destitution and desperation."

The consequences of censorship have intensified for the past several years. Although statistics show a decrease in the number of people who have been charged with "literary crimes," official numbers hide the fact that violence against authors have increased nationwide. The cause of this statistical anomaly is not overtly complex: should someone be sent to prison, it will attract the attention of human rights watchers, and in turn, affect China's international stature. Using violence to "domesticate" authors requires very little effort from the state; moreover, victims also tend to keep silent about their abuse for fear of further acts of aggression. The Chinese government is becoming more and more like an institutionalised crime organisation.

After the publication of WHAT KIND OF GOD, Zhou Qing went to a restaurant with three other friends to celebrate its completion. When Zhou Qing went to the bathroom, three men appeared out of nowhere. In the following moment, they used bottles to beat him unconscious. After they were done with him, they locked Zhou Qing in a bathroom stall. His friends only discovered the wounded Zhou Qing after they saw a trail of blood leaking out from under the door. Zhou Qing received thirty-two stitches due to lacerations to his face. What is truly frightening to this incident is what happened at the police station afterwards.

When Zhou Qing went to the local police station in order to report the assault, the police officer merely shrugged at his report and just said the following:

"You are not one of our own."

To Zhou Qing, this very moment defined the difference between independent writers and state-employed writers: he does not qualify for any police protection because he is simply not affiliated with the state. Whenever someone asked him about his facial scars, he could only meekly answer that it was the result of a traffic accident. Should Zhou Qing put his grievances out in the open, he would have only risked his career as a writer and journalist.

However, at the time, Zhou Qing had another reason to remain silent on this matter: if he told the truth, it would have likely impeded his investigation of the Three Gorges Dam Project.

For his book on the Three Gorges Dam, Zhou Qing would interview the locals who were forced to relocate. When the police received news of his project, the police detained Zhou Qing for more than twenty hours at the local police station. They also turned to potential interview candidates, demanding them to refrain from talking with a man who went by the name of Zhou Qing. The literal words of the police were:

"The moment you open the door for this man, you will be selling out your own country."

According to Zhou Qing, one of the locals gave an especially feisty response to this order:

"How can we sell our country when it is not even ours to begin with? You are the very ones selling out the country!"

This reply poignantly sums up the anger and frustration of the people subject to the whims and control of the state.

_ Lies and truth

"Lies" and "violence" are two key instruments of the Chinese government as readers will know by now. As we have already discussed the use of state violence in the previous section, we will further elaborate on how the Chinese state uses lies to deceive and misguide the public.

While in prison, Zhou Qing was completely dumbfounded when he read the following headline in a newspaper:

"The government hereby declared that all people involved in the Tiananmen-incident have been freed from the prison."

Zhou Qing was shocked at the absurdity of this news article because his fellow inmates were the very students and teachers who had participated in the protest movement.

Zhou Qing felt urged to reveal the truth to the world. Stating the truth is something that Zhou Qing has lived and stood by for over twenty years.

It is normal to feel apprehensive at hearing something called "the truth." From the perspective of the Chinese state—and the party—the truth can potentially unravel their firm control on society. The public fears the truth, because it can have potentially harmful consequences on their livelihood and present living condition; thus, they will maintain a silent conspiracy—as discussed in Chapter 1 - Ran Yunfei. A citizen would harm his family and lose his career, whereas an author will risk imprisonment; and government officials can even lose their lives. Imprisoned authors and lawyers often do not dare speak of their experiences behind the prison walls. Should they expose the truth, it is likely that the police will threaten their family. This is the harsh reality facing the people who live in an authoritarian state.

Zhou Qing reckons that it has become increasingly difficult to reveal the truth in contemporary China. The political atmosphere was relatively relaxed before 1989: publishing was not as constrained and scholars could discuss social and political problems in relative freedom. However, after the Tiananmen-incident in 1989, everything had changed. Whenever someone tries to address public issues—such as the SARS epidemic, the Wenchuan earthquake, or the melamine milk-scandal—then he or she will inevitably be confronted with official "red tape." Should you mind your own business and remain within the confines of your personal space, the state will refrain from interfering with your life. However, should you concern yourself with society, then the government will resolutely show a "STOP!" sign with no exceptions allowed.

_ The Chinese book industry

It is a public secret that all publishing houses in China are under government control. There is, however, one type of publishing house that remains out of government hands, the so-called "private book companies." Run by entrepreneurs, these private book companies are an existence that the communist party wants to place under strict control.

It can be said that the communist party of China and book-publishing industry have always had a love-hate affair with each other. The party adores publishing because small publishers have played a pivotal role in the establishment and development of the Communist Party of China. The party could disseminate its underground publications, such as THE COMMUNIST MANIFESTO, because small and independent publishing houses would publish pro-communist works that helped further cement the power base of the communist party.

The publishing industry became of utmost importance to the party's propaganda work. After the communist party had asserted their dominance in China, the party immediately placed all publishing houses under its control. The party wanted to prevent any rivalling group from hindering their interests. This led to prohibiting private publishing houses and any other political parties that were not affiliated with the communist party.

This has led to the present situation, where starting a publishing company means that you are essentially trying to compete with the communist party. The party is deeply aware of the discursive power of propaganda and literature. From the moment you fund a private book company, the party will have you under close scrutiny; your background or identity has no bearing on this matter. This very fact has spelt trouble for many private book companies, such as for the two entrepreneurs responsible for *Bizarre Sexual Customs*. Because they wanted to venture in the doubly sensitive topics of "ethnic minorities" and "sexuality," both owners were criminally prosecuted.

One of the owners was sentenced to life imprisonment, whereas the other was sentenced to fifteen years in prison. Zhou Qing knows the latter person and is willing to testify for the man's moral character. He reveals that the man used to be a cart driver and is nothing but an upstanding citizen. The man had once heard that he could make some money in the publication industry; thus, he started borrowing money from his family and friends in order to start his private book company with a partner. However, the first issue of *Bizarre Sexual Customs* did not even see its release date before he had found himself in dire straits. People who were only remotely related to the publication were punished and sent to prison. The state even sentenced the editor of an unaffiliated publisher to forty days of prison, because he told the company where they could find a typesetter. If the state is willing to sentence such people to prison, it could in fact happen to anyone else.

Bizarre Sexual Customs became a warning for others who may attempt a similar "act of transgression." The state oppresses these alternative publications in order to prevent people from deviating from the official discourse. The state will not stop at just the destruction a publication, but they will destroy the very lives of common people.

Apart from controlling and suppressing private book companies, the state has another way of strangling and limiting their influence, namely through the system of book identification numbers. As discussed in "Chapter 1 - Ye Fu," you need an identification number in order to publish in China. That makes identification numbers a very valuable commodity in China. If a private book company wants to buy a book identification number they need to spend a small fortune to buy a series of numbers.

Authors who cannot afford book identification numbers can go off the beaten track and choose to publish in Hong Kong. The book stores in Hong Kong will even sell banned books in China. Should the Chinese public want to read banned works, they can cross the border control of Shenzhen and buy the book in Hong Kong. However, this method is not without its risks. The Chinese border patrol equates smuggling banned books to smuggling drugs—it is a so-called "intellectual poison." Should you get caught, you will be sentenced to hard labour for one year.

The public used to know exactly what book is banned as the state would make a public announcement concerning the news. However, this approach led to severe criticisms from commentators in the west. China has learnt from this since then. Instead of publicly announcing book bans it opts for a more subtle approach: government officials simply make a phone call to a bookstore to notify which book should "disappear" from the book shelves.

Before soon, the banned work will be gone from every bookstore in the nation. It has now become impossible for anyone to know what books are banned.

_ The author's duty

Zhou Qing continues walking down the path of an investigative writer. With one pen in the hand and a voice recorder in the other, he tries addressing China's manifold problems.

In a society that lacks freedom and is filled with lies and violence, Zhou Qing is of the opinion that an intellectual needs to have an absolutely clear conscience. This is a prerequisite for authors who want to make a meaningful contribution to the lives of people and the healthful development of society.

/ CHAPTER 3
STATE-EMPLOYED AUTHORS

/ JIA PINGWA

_ The master and his works

Jia Pingwa is a name that you will often see in the Chinese literary world. A state-employed author, Jia Pingwa's ABANDONED CAPITAL, TURBULENCE and QIN QIANG remain famous works among Chinese readers. I have first heard of his work when my high school teacher advised us not to read his books. I did not think much of these words at first, but I finally understood my teacher's meaning after I had started paying more attention to the media and noticed the news concerning Jia Pingwa and his works.

Jia Pingwa (1952) was born in Shaanxi province. After graduating from the literature department of Northwest University, he became an editor at *Chang'an*—a monthly literary magazine of Shaanxi People's Publishing House. In the early 1980s, he became a professional writer when he transferred to the "Shanxi Literary Federation." Jia Pingwa is currently the chairman of the Shaanxi Writers' Association and the Xi'an Literary Federation and holds an undisputed position in Chinese literature. However, in the early 1990s, he had experienced a fair amount of troubles following the controversy of ABANDONED CAPITAL.

_ The controversy of ABANDONED CAPITAL

ABANDONED CAPITAL takes place in the fictitious city of Xijing during one China's eras of transformation, the 1980s. Xijing was once the former capital of a Chinese empire of the past, but due to various historical reasons it has become an ordinary urban city in West-China. In the opening part of the book, Zhou Min—a youth from the city Tongguan—elopes with his lover Tang Wan'er to Xijing. Through personal introductions, the young lovers come to know the famous author Zhuang Zhidie. We read the ups and downs of the book's main characters and how they slowly lose their moral compass through their interactions. Their amoral lives and tragic deaths become symbolically intertwined with the fate of the decaying city of Xijing. Although the once-prosperous city remains, it has become a barren wasteland devoid of life.

Jia Pingwa's novel ABANDONED CAPITAL immediately captured the attention of the Chinese public when it was serialised in the magazine *October* during its six-month run in 1993. When the publisher released the story in book form after the serialisation had ended, the initial print run had been set to five hundred thousand copies. Jia Ping still has fond memories of this period when the novel was at the peak of its success. Entire bookstores would be filled with copies of ABANDONED CAPITAL and news kiosk vendors were scrambling to obtain copies directly from the publisher just so they can put their own copy of ABANDONED CAPITAL up for public display. However, praise soon turned into criticism following the release of ABANDONED CAPITAL: A COMPLETE COLLECTION OF ESSAYS ON JIA PINGWA—a collection of criticisms against Jia Pingwa and his work.

Critics started to deride his writings as "counterrevolutionary" and "decadent," which were labels that would normally sound the death knell for any aspiring author in China.

Within the span of several months, Jia Pingwa transformed from China's most popular author into its most vilified author. The controversy took its toll on Jia Pingwa's mind and body and he felt his health declining. Faced with a weak constitution and a hostile environment, Jia Pingwa saw no other choice but to leave Xi'an. Jia Pingwa sought refuge in a rural village in order to recuperate and dodge the vitriolic attacks of the media. Through a friend's recommendation he found work at a local school. What he could not have imagined at the time was that slander about ABANDONED CAPITAL had even spread to the rural parts of China. The notice boards of the village would be plastered with news clippings about discussions of his book. Even the newspapers he would take with him to relax by the river would also be filled with critiques on his work.

The controversy continued to wage on with no sign of stopping. This finally prompted the state to prohibit all discussion on the once praised and much-beloved ABANDONED CAPITAL—six months after its publication. The Beijing division of the General Administration of Press and Publication was responsible for issuing the ban and condemned the book for its "low standards" and "pornographic descriptions of sex." The publishing house was levied with a fine of one million RMB and the managing editor of the book also lost his early retirement package.

What was the cause for ABANDONED CAPITAL to be so loved and derided? Let us examine the criticism first. Critics derided ABANDONED CAPITAL for three things:

1 Low standards: the story is filled with description of sex; 2 Misogyny: it purposely warps the image of women;
3 Deception: it misleads readers, leading them to think of inappropriate thoughts.

The first two points of criticism point to the characterisation and general plots of the book. However, these two aspects arguably did not bother the readers initially considering the early success of the book. The success of the book lies with the third point of criticism: what intrigued readers was not the intricately composition of the book or the loose values of its characters; it was the stylistic trick Jia Pingwa used in his work. During love scenes, Jia Pingwa would often add blank boxes (   ). This minimalist style of writing stimulated the imagination of its readers to no end. Trying to decipher what is originally written inside those white boxes had become an overnight national pastime. Some readers have even theorised that the white boxes distinguished the pirated version from the official version:

"In order to get approval for the publication, the author must have had to delete all the graphic description of the love scenes."

The truth is actually less spectacular than what his readers have suspected. Jia Pingwa revealed the secret behind of the blank boxes during an interview in 2006. While it is true that he originally had deleted some of the details, Jia Pingwa was already considering the stringent guidelines towards descriptions of sex. The publisher did make some alterations; however, at some point in the writing process, Jia Pingwa decided to directly write boxes. As for the words that he originally envisioned for the blank boxes, Jia Ping admitted that he had already forgotten what these were and lost count of the total deletions—he was already subconsciously censoring the words in his book. The irony of this story is that Jia Pingwa's self-censorship has caused the imagination of his readers to run wild, provoked his critics and it probably caused the ban.

The official version of ABANDONED CAPITAL disappeared from the bookstores, but the pirated version of the book continued to exist. The novel remained popular in spite of its prohibition and detractors: an estimate of the total sale of pirated versions would probably number at least twelve million copies sold. These are such staggering numbers that Jia Pingwa already does not raise his eyebrow anymore when readers hold up a pirated version for him to sign during public events. From time to time, he will also buy the pirated versions for nostalgia's sake; he currently possesses sixty different copies of ABANDONED CAPITAL.

Jia Pingwa never became a *persona non grata* in the literary world of China because of ABANDONED CAPITAL. He also remained a member of the Chinese Writers' Association and continued to publish in China. Nevertheless, this does not mean that the trials and suffering he had endured for writing ABANDONED CAPITAL were anything but trivial. Furthermore, the success of the pirated version of his book would often leave a bitter taste in his mouth and the long controversy concerning ABANDONED CAPITAL aggravated his already weak constitution. Nevertheless, ABANDONED CAPITAL received much international attention due to this controversy. It has been translated into Japanese, Korean, French, Russian, English and won one of France's important literature awards in 1997—the Prix Femina Étranger. Jia Pingwa had become more careful with his public appearances and decided to abstain from the award ceremony. Even when the French Ministry of Culture and Communication bestowed him with the title "Knight of Art and Literature," Jia Pingwa only accepted the decoration from the French ambassador at Northwest University, Xi'an. The Chinese media would often mention that Jia Pingwa has won the Prix Femina Étranger prize, but they would conveniently leave out any mention of ABANDONED CAPITAL. The only exception would be *China Reading Weekly*—a literary newspaper of the General Administration of Press and Publication—that mentioned ABANDONED CAPITAL among the laureates of French literature prizes.

ABANDONED CAPITAL has cast a long shadow over the writing career of Jia Pingwa. Friends have alienated him because of the book and Jia Pingwa has been forced to seclude himself in the rural backcountry of China. Even now, its influence has not totally disappeared from his later work. Jia Pingwa does not touch upon the subject of intellectuals and urbanites anymore; instead, he has focused on the troubles of migrant rural workers labouring in urban areas. Although he can compose in relative freedom now, there is no doubt that Jia Pingwa has imposed some restriction on his writing. Some literary critics argued that if ABANDONED CAPITAL has not been banned, it is likely that Jia Pingwa would have written in a more unrestrained manner.

_ To reprint or to unban: the (un)changing censorship system

Sixteen years after the ban, news came of an official reprint of ABANDONED CAPITAL in 2009 by the Writers' Publishing House. When Jia Pingwa received a sample copy, he could not help but smile and approve of the alluring pink-coloured cover of the book. After being separated for sixteen years, Jia Pingwa could finally meet his beloved brainchild again. However, his enthusiasm soon made place for anxiety.

What ensued was an onslaught of frenzied calls, messages and emails from the media after news of the possibility of a reprint broke out. Jia Pingwa turned off his computer and his telephone in desperation. Worried and helpless, he was preoccupied with the following thought:

"What do you expect me to say? If the situation grows any bigger, the book will be banned again before you'll know it!"

Sensing the possibility of starting yet another controversy, the Writers' Publishing House adopted a careful stance in response. Furthermore, the responsible editor diplomatically told reporters that "the reprint has passed the examination of the General Administration of Press and Publication and would not see any deletions."

When comparing the new edition and the original edition side-by-side, we can hardly see any changes to the content, even the word count and page total are virtually identical. The only notable difference is the change of the mysterious blank boxes (   ) to (…); the latter being less eye-catching than the former. Was the ban lifted on the original or was only the reprint allowed? The answer might not be that relevant since the end result is the same: ABANDONED CAPITAL has an official publication again. The reprint is to allow Jia Pingwa to regain recognition and commercial success for his work. Not only did the work appear in serialised form again along with his other work, the publisher also released single book editions of ABANDONED CAPITAL.

Many people, including Jia Pingwa, attribute the release of the new edition to the enormous changes in China. Values have shifted, whereas things that were once unacceptable in the past have become the norm now. The literary environment is also considerably less constrained: critics tend to judge literature more on its artistic merits instead of focusing on its moral qualities. Although society has changed, censorship in China still happens in an ad-hoc manner. What has probably been pivotal in the re-release of ABANDONED CAPITAL was the fact that the managing state administration changed from the Beijing division to the main division of the General Administration of Press and Publication.

However, the standard to which ABANDONED CAPITAL was held in the 1990s can still be cause for other works of literature to be banned. Authors can still only guess what is acceptable and what is not. While they can learn this through trial-and-error, censorship rules are often subject to continuously changing policies. What is acceptable for one work can suddenly be unacceptable for another work.

_ Writing and staying close to reality

In Jia Pingwa's opinion, an author needs to have the courage to write about reality. Coming across forbidden topics or taboos is normal in China; you just need to make a judgement on what is possible and not. Jia Pingwa will also wonder about the potential ramifications of his work; nevertheless he will try his utmost to write down the things he sees in front of his eyes and stay as close to reality as possible. Finding publication and exploring what is permissible is just the next step in the writing process.

Jia Pingwa observes that many contemporary authors in China tend to deviate from reality in their work. They do not go out into society themselves, nor do they observe and participate in it; they will only rely on official media reports and the fictitious. This causes a divorce between their work and reality; thus, harming the credibility of their work and ultimately turning it into a farce. However, Jia Pingwa does not think that each author is ideally suited to fighting for the freedom of expression. He states that there are essentially two kinds of people:

1 those who are better at handling certain problems; and
2 people who are bad at handling those problems.

Jia Pingwa modestly states that he belongs to the latter category. He has neither the physical prowess nor the ability to confront these kinds of complex problems. That is why he refrains from voicing his personal views in public, only limiting his opinion to the literary domain. The most important thing for him at the moment is to silently continue writing with a calm demeanour.

Jia Pingwa likens literature to a kind of weapon: it can stand up for the weak; however, it can also come into conflict with society. All authors harbour the silent hope that the lives of the people will somehow improve through their writing. Literature still has that special purpose in China.

_ Jia Pingwa versus Mian Mian

At the end of this text, let us compare the authors Jia Pingwa and Mian Mian. Both authors have experienced state prohibition for almost the same reasons, yet their similarities are only limited to their work. We can see that their individual behaviour and values have played a role in the development of their career in China.

When Jia Pingwa received a ban, he decided to retreat to a rural village while waiting for the situation to calm down. Mian Mian, conversely, rode on the publicity of her ban and travelled around the globe in order to promote her work. Mian Mian's international presence is the very opposite of Jia Pingwa's modest behaviour. This is perhaps the crucial difference between these two authors. In the eyes of state officials, Mian Mian is akin to an incorrigible repeat offender: Mian Mian's work continues to have problems with censorship in her home country. This has caused the following difference between these authors: Jia Pingwa has an ever-growing presence in the Chinese literature world, whereas Mian Mian has remained relatively obscure.

Of course, this comparison would yield different results with other authors. Then, there is also the fact that Jia Pingwa is a state-employed author, whereas Mian Mian is an independent writer. The Chinese government is probably the only entity who can tell us the reasons behind the censorship of an author. However, should you directly ask for a specific reason, it is likely that you will hear the answer that authors will often from state officials:

"You'd probably understand your own situation better than we do."

/ YAN LIANKE

Yan Lianke is known as one of China's most controversial authors. Numerous books of his have been banned, yet he has received an even greater number of awards and accolades. His works are known to be notoriously difficult to publish in the publication industry.

Although he is "controversial," Yan Lianke's writing talent is undeniable. It has propelled him into the stratosphere of China's literary sphere, where he reigns as one of the giants of contemporary literature. There is universal consensus in the Chinese literary world, that Yan Lianke is the most likely candidate from China to receive a Nobel Prize in Literature after Mo Yan—Nobel laureate in Literature of 2012. What is the story behind this author whose every movement has caused waves in the literary world?

Yan Lianke (1958) was born to a poor family. His ancestral home is a small mountain village called Tianhu village in Song County, Henan province. Raised on the mountains of Balou, Yan Lianke lived a hardworking childhood in the rural backcountry of China. Later in his career, Yan Lianke would retrace his footsteps and use his place of birth as an important source of inspiration.

When Yan Lianke started high school in 1972, he began reading novels. As the Cultural Revolution was at its peak during that time, Yan Lianke mainly read communist literature. In 1975, Yan Lianke read a book called DEMARCATION LINE that left a huge impact on him. Although he does not remember the exact contents of the book anymore, what impressed the young Yan Lianke was the few hundred words introducing the author on the back cover. Yan Lianke learnt from these words that the author could move from the rural areas of Beidahuang to Harbin city because of writing that specific novel. This awakened Yan Lianke to the power and attraction of writing. At the time, he would work tirelessly on the fields under the scorching heat of the sun, day after day. His heart and mind were filled with the desire to live in the city and quit the monotonous, yet arduous rural lifestyle. He had never imagined that writing a novel would present such a chance.

Shocked to the core of his being, the young Yan Lianke made up his mind and started to write in his spare time. Whenever his family would be sleeping, he would sit down with an oil lamp by his side and write for three to four hours straight. He had written more than hundred thousand words before his mother destroyed his efforts.

His mother thought his manuscript was trash and burned his young ambition in the incinerator.

Yan Lianke continued writing after he was conscripted into the army and became a platoon leader. If he did not continue to write, then he would have to return home after his military service was over. Wanting to change his destiny, he had published a short-story in the Wuhan military journal *Battle Report* in 1979. This proved to be the turning point in his life, as his publication allowed him to enter the literature department of the People's Liberation Army Arts College. He could finally say goodbye to his rural lifestyle and set out on the path to become a writer.

Yan Lianke would make the transition from military man to becoming a writer of the Chinese Writers' association before finally becoming a lecturer at the literature department of Renmin University (Beijing). While writing has given Yan Lianke a chance to personally change his future, it has also forced him to deal with censorship.

_ The defamation of XIA RILUO

The novel XIA RILUO was written in 1993 and published in 1994. Yan Lianke had offered his manuscript at various magazines, but none were willing to publish his work. One year had passed before the literary magazine *Yellow River* finally released the story.

The story is about the soldier Xia Riluo. Xia steals a gun from his regiment and uses it to commit suicide. The senior officers decide to investigate the cause of his death by interrogating the regiment leader and instructor. However, both people start to shift blame on each other during the interrogation in order to dodge responsibility. Their behaviour only causes the senior leadership to put them together in a confinement room. While the two men are sitting out their detainment, they hear news that Vietnam has re-established diplomatic ties with China—twelve years after the Sino-Vietnamese war. This prompts the two men to reminisce about the war as they have both fought on the war-torn grounds of Vietnam. After they have reflected on the war and the many comrades who sacrificed themselves, they realise the error of their ways.

The story attracted a lot of critique after its release: critics accused Yan Lianke of desecrating the noble image of the military. Yan Lianke response to these criticisms was that he only wanted to write a simple story depicting ordinary army men; it is not a military epic depicting the struggles of some patriotic hero. However, Yan Lianke had committed a *faux pas* by turning military men into ordinary people and describing the ground view of a battlefield. This resulted in a ban on the book, just three months after its publication. Yan Lianke, who had just moved from Henan province to join "Beijing's Second Artillery Creative Room," had to undergo half a year of self-criticism as soon as he arrived at his new unit. The matter died down after this probation period.
Yan Lianke has walked a thorny publication road since XIA RILUO. The debacle of XIA RILUO caused Yan Lianke to lose his passion for the military genre; instead, China's

rural life became his main subject. Nevertheless, his troubles with censorship did not end at that point.

_ Revolution and sex in AS HARD AS WATER and SERVE THE PEOPLE!

The novel AS HARD AS WATER is set during the Cultural Revolution. The reservist Gao Aijun returns home to join the Cultural Revolution and, subsequently, falls in love with a local woman. While they participate in the Cultural Revolution, Gao Aijun and his lover constantly indulge in lovemaking at seemingly every possible place, such as grave sites and abandoned tunnels. What is remarkable about their intercourse is that it becomes more frenzied whenever they can hear the Red Guards' singing in the background. The more uplifting the beat was, the stronger their lust would be for each other. After the Cultural Revolution comes to an end, the two lovers end up in prison for being accomplishes in the mass movement. They have become sacrificial pawns in the political aftermath of the Cultural Revolution.

Yan Lianke makes a mockery of the Cultural Revolution in his book AS HARD AS WATER. He links the violent behaviour of its participants with a primal instinct for sex: the protagonist Gao Aijun did not have any physical contact with the opposite sex for a long period of time, yet he could fully release his long repressed desires during the Cultural Revolution. The subliminal message here is that whatever drove the Cultural Revolution causes the two protagonists into feeling constant lust for each other. This symbolism is even more pronounced when they make love in the most dark and decrepit places surrounded by violence and base desires. This linkage and contrast have undoubtedly destroyed the public image of the Cultural Revolution when the story saw release.

As soon as the book saw publication, the Propaganda Department as well as the General Administration of Press and Publication received a petition letter decrying the heresy and perverse nature of the book. The letter further claimed that Yan Lianke violated communist principles as well as public morals. In the ensuing controversy that erupted, the head editor of the publishing house had to personally go to Beijing in order to manage the situation. After treating several important figures to dinner and tea, he could finally calm down the situation. The head editor only received one direct instruction: "you may publish the book, but you cannot advertise it." These consequences were fairly mild, especially when compared to the fallout of SERVE THE PEOPLE!

Yan Lianke's next novel SERVE THE PEOPLE! takes the iconoclasm of AS HARD AS WATER to the next level. It narrates the love affair between an army attendant and the spouse of his superior. The couple uses Mao Zedong's iconic slogan "Serve the people!" as a password for their adultery. One day, the army attendant suddenly becomes impotent.

However, the adulterous couple find out that the man will regain his virility whenever they smash sculptures of Mao Zedong into pieces. Thus, their relationship takes on an obsessive new dimension where they find their sex life being stimulated by the wanton destruction of Mao's likeness.

In SERVE THE PEOPLE!, Yan Lianke directly aimed his sights at the very status of Mao Zedong, such as turning the much vaunted slogan of "Serve the people!" into a secret sign for adulterous love-making. Yan Lianke finished the novel while he was still in the army. However, after considering his obligations at the time, he wisely decided to refrain from immediate publication until his military service was over. The literary magazine *Harvest* was supposed to publish the work, but they retracted their offer after an internal deliberation. The manuscript was then sent to Huacheng Publishing; however, the magazine only managed to print the first half of the story before the state administration put a stop to the publication. A gag order was placed on the work, forbidding any other publication from publishing the story. Two weeks later, a joint statement came from the Central Propaganda Department and the General Administration of Press and Publication. The statement declared that the following six prohibitions were placed on the book:

_ prohibited from circulation;
_ prohibited from reprinting;
_ prohibited from discussion;
_ prohibited from extracts or abstracts;
_ prohibited from reports;
_ prohibited from sale (prints already in circulation must be recalled and destroyed).

Official bans are usually orally transmitted in order to prevent leaving a paper trail; an instruction on paper has not been seen since the Cultural Revolution. The joint statement was spread across the whole nation and even reached the rural home of Yan Lianke in the Balou Mountains. Yan Lianke's reputation as a "controversial author" had proved true once again.

This time, the chairman of the Chinese Writers' Association had to personally get involved in order to prevent the situation from further spiralling out of control. The chairman managed to exonerate Yan Lianke by pointing out that Yan Lianke finished the novel while he was in the army, but refrained from publishing immediately. He also guaranteed that this will not happen again in the future. Once again, Yan Lianke had somehow passed another official examination.

In his recollections of the affair, Yan Lianke stated that he was under considerable pressure at the time. Furthermore, he felt sorry for implicating his friends, the publishing house and the magazine in this controversy. However, this very novel has brought Yan Lianke international fame in hindsight, as it was his first novel to be translated in English. It remains his most popular work to date; whenever he goes abroad, it is almost inevitable that people will start asking about his book SERVE THE PEOPLE!

_ THE JOY OF LIVING: From army man to citizen

Yan Lianke's novel THE JOY OF LIVING is titled after the fictional Shouhuo village—a village that is almost entirely cut off from society. Although nearly all of its inhabitants are invalids, they possess unique talents and soon form a touring theatrical company. Under the guidance of the main protagonist Liu Yingque, they find great success when they leave the village to perform in the outside world. The discrepancy between "normal people" and the "disabled" becomes more and more apparent as the story unfolds. This very contrast forms the basis of Yan Lianke's critique of contemporary Chinese society. The story describes how public morals have withered away in the process of national modernisation and reveals the weaknesses in a society that blindly pursues material wealth. Bullying the weak and fearing the strong have become the standard and self-worth is worthless in the face of money. Some people lose contact with reality to the point that they that cannot wake up from their delusions of splendour, even when their own personal well-being is at stake.

As soon as THE JOY OF LIVING was released in 2003, the Central Propaganda Department convened an emergency meeting. The result of the meeting: "in order to avoid drawing unnecessary publicity to the book with a ban, the decision has been made to allow a silent release; the media and the publishing house are forbidden from marketing and discussing the book."

Yan Lianke was still working for the army when he wrote the story. His senior officers foresaw the potential trouble that Yan Lianke would attract with THE JOY OF LIVING when they read the story; therefore, they made arrangements to expel him from the army. At the time, Yan Lianke was interviewed on Phoenix TV to promote his work. The day following the interview session, his platoon leader commended Yan Lianke for his television performance. He told Yan Lianke that the senior staff had taken his future career path into consideration and concluded that the army might hinder his further development. The senior leadership has therefore made the decision that Yan Lianke should request a formal transfer to the civilian sector. In a reconstruction of the events, Yan Lianke had handed in his request at one o' clock afternoon. Within an hour, Yan Lianke received a telephone call, notifying that all of his eight senior officers have approved his request. The army had allowed him three days to find new employment.

The transfer did not differ much from being directly expelled from the army. At that point, Yan Lianke had already resigned himself to heading home for Henan province.

However, on the second day of his unemployment, he had the fortune to meet with the Chairman of the Beijing Writers' Association during dinner. The two immediately hit off on a good note and Yan Lianke had found new employment. Yan Lianke made the switch from army man to professional writer.

_ The naked truth of DREAM OF DING VILLAGE

The 2005 novel DREAM OF DING VILLAGE was Yan Lianke's first foray in pursuing a more realist style. The story touches on the AIDS-scandal in Henan province during the 1990s. The province saw the rise of a clandestine business in selling blood transfusions on a large scale. The poor sold their blood in order to escape poverty; however, the blood transfusions had happened in a careless and slovenly manner. As a result, entire villages contracted the AIDS-virus; thus, forcing the provincial government to quarantine the infected population. The people of Henan province ended paying a dear price for engaging in such risky business.

Yan Lianke secretly investigated an AIDS-struck village seven times in order to collect data for his book. He interviewed many of the locals to get an idea of the situation. The national news also covered the tragedy at the time, but the village Yan Lianke visited was even worse than the reports. After personally hearing the stories from the mouths of the villagers, Yan Lianke decided to write it all down on paper in order to spread the word. For that reason, DREAM OF DING VILLAGE can be said to be Yan Lianke's most realistic novel at the time.

The book not only highlights the problem with medical hygiene in China but also relates the AIDS epidemic to problems with the national economy, social welfare and government corruption. Yan Lianke describes the evil and ugly sides of politics and business, and shows that politicians and businessmen simply do not care about the fate of ordinary citizens. Yan Lianke opted to focus on the human tragedy in his story in order to prevent another confrontation with the state censors. This perspective might be limiting in some ways, but Yan Lianke still manages to capture the inherent problems in Chinese society.

Nevertheless, the state censors banned the book three days after its release in spite of Yan Lianke's best efforts. Apparently, Yan Lianke may not write a report on the AIDS-epidemic in China, because this right only belongs to official news outlets. Yan Lianke could only sigh in resignation when confronted with this fact.

_ ELEGY AND ACADEME the book that angered Chinese intellectuals

In his 2008 novel ELEGY AND ACADEME, Yan Lianke wrote a novel about hypocrisy and corrupt practises at universities, where influence can buy anything. Once again, Yan Lianke managed to attract a large amount of criticism. His critics complain that Yan Lianke's book is a scathing attack on the prestigious Peking University—one of the top universities in China—and deride him for writing an incredulous story, while he himself lacks any first-hand knowledge of university life:

"This is nothing but a defamatory work that attacks the university and the very nature of higher education."

When Jiangsu People's Publishing House published the book, the publishers used the following promotional tag line:

"Already attracting nationwide controversy even before it is even released to the public!"

Many publishers had passed on the manuscript before the book arrived at Jiangsu People's Publishing House. Among the publishers who had passed on the book, there was one publisher who contracted the book but backed out at the last moment. When Yan Lianke asked about their reasons, the publisher merely stated that they were unable to publish the book. When he pressed on, the publisher replied that he should not ask about the details.

The Writers' Publishing House also agreed with a publication, but requested a dozen edits to his manuscript. Yan Lianke made sixteen modifications before he realised that he could not fulfil the last two requirements:

1 The tone of the whole story was too gloomy; therefore he should "lighten" the mood
2 All the characters were flawed in some way; Yan Lianke needed to write a character without flaws.

Even at his eventual publisher—Jiangsu People's Publishing House—Yan Lianke still had to make countless revisions to his manuscript before it was accepted. Yan Lianke consoled himself during the editorial process by thinking the following:

"If you want me to edit, then I'll edit; if you want me to delete then I'll delete. In any case, I'll publish the unedited edition in Taiwan."

_ The hidden history of China in CHRONICLES OF ZHALIE and FOUR BOOKS
The novel CHRONICLES OF ZHALIE was published in 2013 by Shanghai Literature Art Publishing House. The novel is a historic retelling of the rapidly developing Chinese society after the Economic Reforms. Yan Lianke projects thirty years of Chinese contemporary history through the lens of the fictional Zhalie Village. Yan Lianke's story discusses the downsides to the economic reforms, and describes how enmity, sex, money and power can affect a rural society such as Zhalie Village.

Yan Lianke initially wondered whether his new novel would pass the publication process unscathed, because the book is set in reality. Yan Lianke uses exaggerates events to put some distance between fiction and reality in order to prevent another ban. His efforts paid off in the end as the book did not cause a controversy after its official release. This was different for his other historical work FOUR BOOKS.

FOUR BOOKS the book saw no release in China before it saw publication in Taiwan in 2013. No publisher was willing to release the book in China, because the book was set during the Great Leap Forward. Yan Lianke went to eighteen different publishers in China, before giving up on the domestic market. The Taiwanese version would have the next promotional line splashed over its cover:

"Something that only Yan Lianke would dare to write: the legendary banned work that could not find publication in China!

Yan Lianke has once stated that he writes without constraints. He admits that there is a side to him that is eager to see an actual publication of his books, but he would never write just for the sake of publication. He would not chose to censor himself out of choice. It is almost an inevitable law that mandates authors to compromise if they want to publish their book in China. However, Yan Lianke chose not to compromise with FOUR BOOKS. Many authors have opted for the same thing as Yan Lianke and all have shared the same mind-set:

"Having one Chinese version is already enough, where it gets published is of second interest."

_ The creative poverty of China
Yan Lianke notes that it is wrong to assume that all banned books are good examples of literature when talking about the creative environment of China. Any author or work can suffer an official criticism or a ban, even those who regularly praise the communist party in their work. However, when we look at it from a different perspective, receiving a ban just from writing a book is also something abnormal.

Yan Lianke had to write self-criticisms for half a year when his first anti-war novel XIA RILUO saw release in 1994. When his novel AS HARD AS WATER came out in 2000, people reported the book to the state administration, claiming it was vulgar and violating communist principles. His 2005 novel SERVE THE PEOPLE! touched on similar themes and caused even greater waves. The work also had the dubious honour of being the first book since the Cultural Revolution to receive an almost instantaneous ban after its release. After his book THE JOY OF LIVING came out in 2003, the Central Propaganda Department convened a special meeting and forbade the media from discussing the book. DREAM OF DING VILLAGE, which investigated the AIDS-problem in Henan, received a ban just three days after its public release in 2005. His 2008 novel ELEGY AND ACADEME also managed to anger Chinese intellectuals, as the iconoclast book satirises the public image of professors and college life in general. In 2013, his historical work FOUR BOOKS—set during the Great Leap Forward—skipped domestic publication entirely and was only released in Taiwan. That year also saw the release of his other historical novel CHRONICLES OF ZHALIE, which describes the history of China since the Economic Reforms, Yan Lianke was initially not even sure that the work could see release but the famous literary magazine *Harvest* released his work in a special issue and a book edition was later released by the Shanghai Literature Art Publishing House.

Yan Lianke has found out in his many years of writing in China that it is not possible to always have your own way. It is not as if Yan Lianke is unwilling to compromise, but his numerous clashes with the censors would suggest otherwise. It could also mean that Yan Lianke is not very proficient at censoring his work: he is deeply aware of the fact that censorship limits the choices for expression, but that self-censorship is absolutely fatal to an author. Many Chinese authors place a restriction on their writing process in order to dodge problems and some authors even claim that writing in China is done in complete freedom—they claim to be able to write whatever they want. What they do not realise, however, is that self-censorship takes place on a subconscious level; the things they write on paper have already been filtered by their own minds.

Yan Lianke complains that the publishing environment in China has been made unreasonable due to an irrational censorship policy:

"What should be banned does not get a ban; what shouldn't be banned does get banned."

His SERVE THE PEOPLE! and AS HARD AS WATER were both absurdly written, yet only the latter could be sold on the market; the former work was sent into publication hell. Furthermore, THE JOY OF LIVING was a revisionist historic retelling of contemporary history and a quintessential example of an "anti-communist work," but it could still be publicly sold, albeit with some restrictions. What is the reasoning behind such a decision?

Even Yan Lianke does not know the answer to this question.

_ Facing reality while writing

Yan Lianke is of the opinion that authors cannot turn a blind eye to our social reality.

Public discourse might be restricted and heavily regulated in China, but Yan Lianke still manages to write about social issues in spite of these restrictions. The present Chinese reality is extremely complex and absurd on many levels. Therefore, it is essential that authors need to see the world in front of their own eyes and learn how they can engage with social problems before providing a potential solution.

Yan Lianke states that he has the utmost respect for social activists such as Liu Xiaobo, because he has found himself unable to accomplish the same things in the same manner as these people. Yan Lianke can only do his utmost with what he is able to do at the moment. This is Yan Lianke's own answer to his duty as an author: it is to scrutinise society and to reveal its many problems with his pen.

/ YU HUA

_Hanging up the doctor's coat for literature

In these past years, the literary presence of Yu Hua (1960) can be felt all over China and in the international literature world. Yu Hua had practised dentistry for five year after the end of the Cultural Revolution before taking up the pen. He has therefore an interesting commonality with Lu Xun "the godfather of contemporary Chinese literature": both practised medicine, only to give this up in favour of writing. At present, Yu Hua is a professional writer residing in Beijing. He started releasing his first novels from 1984, won many awards and has attained universal acclaim as one of China's leading authors of contemporary literature. Some of his famous works are TO LIVE, BROTHERS and CHINA IN TEN WORDS, a work that Yu Hua only dared to release in Taiwan. Furthermore, Yu Hua is also a featured columnist for the New York Times. His work has been translated into more than twenty different languages and attained a loyal readership overseas. The Swiss newspaper *Le Temps* has ranked his novel BROTHERS as "one of the top 50 important novels in the world of the 2000-2010 period."

_ The naked history and reality

Yu Hua usually sets his stories in modern times while staying close to reality, such as the novels TO LIVE and BROTHERS. Both stories describe the creation of a family and its disintegration during the various (man-made) disasters in China. Yu Hua writes about taboo subjects such as the Three-anti and Five-anti Campaigns; Great Leap Forward; and the Cultural Revolution. Attentive readers should know by now that writing about these historical periods will often attract the scrutiny of the state censors. Therefore, the question is how these two novels could end up for sale in bookstores all over the nation and even become national bestsellers.

Yu Hua's book TO LIVE is about Fu Gui—the son of a wealthy landowner. Growing up in the republican era, his young adulthood is spent debauching and gambling like his life depended on it. In the opening act of the story, Fu Gui manages to gamble away his family fortune. This ordeal enrages his father so much that he actually dies of a stroke. Before he knows it, Fu Gui is working for the national army as a jack-of-all trades and becomes embroiled in the civil war between the republican army and the communist army. He survives through all kinds of political campaigns, such as the "Three-anti and Five-anti Campaigns," "Great Leap Forward" and the "Cultural Revolution" but experiences much bitterness. His family members all end up dying, leaving him alone with only an old cow to keep him company.

BROTHERS begins in an ordinary city called Jiangnan and narrates the story of two brothers—Baldy Li and Song Gang. The two brothers experience the ups and downs of the Cultural Revolution—such as mass mobilisation and collective criticism sessions. A schism appears between the brothers when the Cultural Revolution is over. One becomes successful and rich during the Economic Reforms of China, whereas the other stays true to the ideals of the Cultural Revolution but ends up becoming irrelevant in contemporary China.

As a pioneer in his field, Yu Hua tends to maintain a sober tone in his narrative. His works explore the full spectrum of human ugliness and is filled with cruelty, terror and death. However, if we examine his work in more detail, it is not hard to see that his stories primarily focus on the personal stories of humans and their personal suffering. His work does not pretend to be a historical recollection of the time period itself; it is in fact a story about individuals, their sorrow and the absurdity of their times. Yu Hua might use hyperbole in his stories to further the plot, but he does not criticise history at all, nor does he try to blame anything or anyone for the dramas of that time. The characters in his work are all politically insignificant.

Yu Hua manages to write about the "Cultural Revolution" in TO LIVE and BROTHERS by dispelling its thick political significance while distilling the time period to its core. It could be said that the Cultural Revolution in his work is modelled after his youthful impressions of the time period when he was growing up. This might explain his description of a barbaric and seemingly scary world. Nevertheless, he is also ardently trying to find the meaning behind human kindness and life in general. Looking at it from this perspective, Yu Hua is writing about the Cultural Revolution and other time pieces, because he wants to stimulate his readers into looking back at historical times—his work is an enquiry of history. This probably makes his work relatively safe to publish in China: Yu Hua does not choose sides in his historical narrative; he only tries to stimulate silent contemplation.

Yu Hua's novel THE SEVENTH DAY is a more direct critique of Chinese society when compared to his previous work. The story narrates seven days of the ghost Yang Fei—a person who died without a proper burial ceremony. Through the narration of the dead Yang Fei, the author severely criticises the problems that have appeared in Chinese society since the Economic Reforms. Yu Hua discusses problems such as "the inability for the poor to bury the dead properly," "forced relocations under pressure of project developers," "the fixation on the outward appearance of women," "the hidden number of rising child deaths," "insecurities on the housing market," "inadequate medical coverage," "illegal prostitution," "illegal trading in organs" and many more. The characters appearing in the story are all in desperate situations. Their very characterisation embodies the despair and grief existent in contemporary society. Yu Hua describes the pains and suffering in his stories with a hint of black humour, he writes in a detached manner to enable sufficient distance between fiction and reality. Yu Hua's mastery over this writing form has probably allowed his book to be published. That is undoubtedly the workings of an "experienced" writer.

_ The freedom of May 35th

In 2011, Yu Hua published a work in Taiwan called CHINA IN TEN WORDS. In the book, Yu Hua used the following keywords to describe the changes in Chinese society during the last few decades:

_People
_ Leadership
_ Reading
_ Composition
_ Lu Xun
_ Inequality
_ Revolution
_ Grassroots
_ Imitation products
_ Deception

When he started writing his first chapter "People," Yu Hua immediately realised that he would not be able to have a domestic release of the book. As it was a non-fiction book, all the things in his book would be fully grounded in reality. Where Yu Hua used to avoid non-fiction in his novels, this time he would directly write about historical issues in his newest work, such as the Tiananmen-incident, which Yu Hua calls the biggest patriotic movement in human history.

The Tiananmen-incident is one of the most delicate keywords in China. It is impossible to mention the word "Tiananmen" or the date of "June 4th, 1989" in any kind of publication regardless of the context wherein it may appear. In order to bypass this problem, a special date appeared in the Chinese public sphere, namely that of May 35th—a reference to June fourth. By referring to the Tiananmen-incident in this indirect way, you can escape censorship, while being able to commemorate the event and discuss its historical significance.

Journalists have asked Yu Hua why BROTHERS can appear in China, whereas CHINA IN TEN WORDS cannot, since both works are set in contemporary China. Yu Hua has replied that this is the difference between fiction and non-fiction works. On the one hand, BROTHERS uses a lot of indirect references and obscure meanings—it has fortunately become one of the works that could escape the gaze of the censors. On the other hand, CHINA IN TEN WORDS is simply too straight-forward and direct, there is no way you can escape censorship. BROTHERS is May 35th, while CHINA IN TEN WORDS is June fourth.

Yu Hua is more than willing to use the May 35th-euphemism as a novelist, as this fictional writing style has allowed him to publish freely in China. However, CHINA IN TEN WORDS is a temporary release from his old story-telling method. Although the Chinese version is only released in Taiwan, Yu Hua is already satisfied that there is a Chinese version for sale on the open market. Readers who want to read his work will be able to find a way to read it.

_ Does China have freedom of expression?

Whenever Yu Hua comes across the following question, namely "does China have any freedom of expression?" Yu Hua will answer:

"Of course, but freedom of expression is relative in any kind of country."

If you want to express your full opinion in China, then you will have to put more effort into your writing. The example of May 35th is one kind of freedom; it is only a bit more refined and indirect than the direct way of expressing June fourth. The Chinese population has already explored the full range of the Chinese language in order to escape censorship. Especially on the Internet, we can see many common words bestowed with new meaning and re-purposed words for subtle satire, subterfuge and exaggeration. The Chinese language is able to reach new levels of subtleties due to these lingual developments; it empowers citizens to give vent to their dissatisfaction.

The word "harmony" is a good example of this. The Chinese government always espouses the concept of "Harmonious Society," but the censors are willing to use any measure to cover up any kind of facts or truths that would go against the government. It is an intolerant stance that is all but harmonious. Therefore, some bright mind has decided to use the word "harmony" in a new fashion: "beware of being harmonised," or rather "take care not to be banned or to be arrested." The government cannot exactly ban the satirical use of the word "harmony" since it is part of their political slogan. The same goes for the innocuous usage of the word "river crab"—a homonym for the word "Harmonious Society." Playing of the fact that these two words sound the same in Chinese, any Chinese seeing the word "River Crab" will immediately understand the reference.

Using such indirect references, anyone can discuss sensitive topics without attracting censorship. In addition to that, there are several layers of humour added to it as Yu Hua would argue:

"If you do not find this amusing in the least bit, then you undoubtedly have a very dry sense of humour."

This cat-and-mouse game with the government has been going on for many years.

Nevertheless, Chinese censors are all but stupid; they will make sure that you will suffer the consequences when you cross a line that should not be crossed.

_ Multi-faceted author and the middle-way

Yu Hua would like to imagine that censors sometimes have a helpless and conflicted expression on their face when they are not being uncaring and inflexible. Censorship guidelines have constantly switched between periods of constraint and flexibility, seemingly without reason or cause. Censors might lift a ban or allow a reprint of the work-in-question when it has already been pirated many times over. Furthermore, censors might allow the publication of a story in book form but forbid it from being adapted into films, even if the story has been a bestselling classic for over twenty years. Yu Hua argues that book bans are not very effective measures in a country where pirated versions often negate the efforts of censors. A ban might even adversely cause people to actively seek out the banned work and download a pirated version from the Internet. Even if these options are absent, one can always go to Hong Kong or Taiwan and buy the local Chinese version. As long as readers are willing to go the extra mile, they will be able to obtain a banned book. The government is well aware of these illegal channels; nevertheless, they still need to adopt official measures for appearance's sake.

Publishers have made use of this phenomenon for their own advantage. The revenues of a publishing house used to come from state funds; however, this has changed when publishing houses were privatised after the Economic Reforms. The responsibility of securing revenue now falls on the head of the publishing house, who has the final say in deciding what works are publishable and what not. It can be said that when a book is rejected by several publishers, there are always other publishers available who are willing to take the risk. Yu Hua argues that political considerations are but a minor risk in the publication industry when compared to the financial incentives of a potential bestseller. It all comes down to the likelihood of a book becoming a bestseller or not in the end. Even when the political risks are great, a courageous publisher might still be willing to take that gamble.

It is possible that these factors have allowed Yu Hua to find success in China, where others have not. He writes fiction in China, publishes non-fiction in Taiwan, and writes editorials in the United States; at different venues, Yu Hua will say different things. I am personally not sure whether Yu Hua professes or walks a middle road, but the answer might not even be that important. What is truly at stake here is the issue of whether an author is able to write about historical and social issues and be able to translate these onto paper. Writing in the wavering yet strict censorship of China, Yu Hua has once stated the following on this issue:

"I think that readers come prepared with a certain ability to reflect and to think. They will be able to find the historical truths hidden within the works of an author. If we can understand our pasts, then we can use that to scrutinise the present and face the future."

/ EPILOGUE

_Well-behaved authors

After discussing eleven authors, we have arrived at the end of the book. There are countless names still floating in the back of my head and they are all state-employed authors of whom I have wanted to dedicate a vignette on. However, when I started investigating these authors in detail, I found out that they were simply too "well-behaved." Although they might have one or two banned books in their library, these authors have refrained from causing any major controversies in China. The bans might have caused them to become even more low-profile in their work: they become wary of their public appearance in public and never dare cross the icy lake of censorship. Most of these authors usually use humour to discuss social issues, but their writing style usually side-lines the real issues. In that situation, authors run the risk that the audience will not take their work serious and pass it off as another piece of humorous fiction.

I will use the author Mai Jia as an example for a popular "well-behaved author." It is not an exaggeration to say that his work and its many adaptations have captured the hearts and minds of the Chinese public, yet his work ultimately shies away from political issues.

After that, I will shortly discuss Liu Zhenyun, whose humour tends to distract from the real issues at hand. Lastly, I will discuss the nameless authors that I have decided not to include in the book.

_ Mai Jia

Mai Jia is a graduate of the Military Engineering Institute of the People's Liberation Army—a clandestine military academy, famous for training intelligence personnel. After graduation, Mai Jia worked at a military intelligence unit before becoming an author. Thanks to his background, Mai Jia is an author with first-hand knowledge in the spy genre. His first long-form novel DECODED is about ciphers breaking secret codes. Published in 2002, the novel went on to win the "Mao Dun Prize" in 2008—one of China's most prestigious literary awards. Even though Mai Jia enjoys commercial and critical success, his background has caused him to come into contact with censorship.

Three months after the publication of DECODED, the General Administration of Press and Publication received an anonymous telephone report. The report stated that the book used classified information for its story. The state promptly issued a ban notice the next day; notifying the whole country that the sale of the book is to be stopped effective immediately. At the time, Mai Jia thought it was preposterous that he would lose eleven years of hard labour, because of one anonymous call. Mai Jia personally went to Beijing to call in some favours, hoping to convince the General Administration of Press and Publication to withdraw the ban. Mai Jia felt that the ban would be justified if the book was in violation of leaking classified secrets, as Mai Jia places priority on the national interests before everything else. Nevertheless, he was convinced that his book was not in violation of any crime. The National Security Bureau and the People's Liberation Army General Staff Department finally conducted another examination of the book, because more than twenty people were willing to testify that the book did not leak any state secret. The ban was lifted a few months later and the book was put up for sale again. Although Mai Jia managed to overturn the decision of the state censors, he needed to jump through many administrative hoops to bring about this result.

Mai Jia admits that he enjoyed a greater degree of leniency thanks to the popularity of American television hit series "House of Cards." This American spy series was at the height of its popularity in China and made it possible for Mai Jia to write a book on the spy genre.

However, writing a novel on countering-intelligence in China is on a separate level of difficulty than broadcasting an American television series on the same subject. Spy thrillers often deal with sensitive topics such as state secrets; therefore, the problem lies with carefully avoiding the "red tape." Mai Jia is of the opinion that you need to use your own judgement and your own creative ingenuity for this purpose:

"It is akin to dancing with your arms and legs chained together. If you manage to dance well, you will pass without fail and proceed to publish your work. Should you do a poor job at it, then your work will be banned and it is likely that you will also put yourself in danger."

Fortunately, Mai Jia has enough familiarity with the subject matter to be able to see when he should back off. He is able to skirt close to classified information, without ever really crossing any boundaries. Furthermore, Mai Jia often coats his work in "red" paint to show his allegiance to the party, state and nation. Doing this, he can please the demands of the government and safeguard his livelihood as an author.

Even now, I feel apprehensive about the work of Mai Jia. While the story of his book ban—and stunning reversal of the decision—is interesting and relevant to this book, Mai Jia fits the quintessential image of a well-behaved author. Self-censorship in the Chinese spy genre is often unavoidable and often results in the warping of historical facts. Mai Jia has used the Cultural Revolution as the background setting for his stories, but a critical reader might walk away with the feeling that the time period was only used in a perfunctory manner. Other contemporary periods such as "Three-anti and Five-anti Campaigns," "Great Leap Forward," and the "Great Famine" have been notably missing in his body of work. Authors such as Mai Jia are simply too "well-behaved." You will find them lacking in credibility, because they always tend to refrain from voicing their true opinion in order not to upset the party. This could be either self-preservation or profit-mindedness. Regardless of the reasons, if I were to devote a whole vignette on authors such as Mai Jia, I would probably only be able to write at most a couple of paragraphs before finding myself unable to continue.

_ Liu Zhenyun

Another author that was on my mind is Liu Zhenyun. His novel I AM NOT PAN JINLIAN is about a girl who goes to submit a petition in the capital and is confronted with uncaring government officials who can only push responsibilities onto others. The book does touch on a sensitive, if not painful issue in China, namely the difficulty in submitting a petition and voicing your complaints to high officials. The problem often lies with the fact that government officials do not always have the best interests of the people at heart.

Unfortunately, Liu Zhenyun mostly uses this premise as a vehicle for humour and hyperbole, but he side-lines the real problem at hand. The work may have only passed the official examination because it gave the censors a good laugh. This is a typical case where the humour actually distracts from the message.

_ The nameless

I also wanted to include people who were my personal friends. They are state-employed authors; and some of them are even quite famous. Whenever I talk to them, I discover to my consternation that they are always careful with their words regardless of the occasion. This causes me to wonder whether their current occupation is sustainable or even suitable for their long-term plans. On several occasion they have made the following statement:

"Literature is literature, why should it mix with politics? Why are state-employed authors always the bad guys? As long as you are a state-employed author, your work will be derided as a product of the party. However, the day when you go independent, you will be praised as an artist, even if the things you write haven't changed."

I have to agree that there is some truth to these words, as some of the criticisms levelled at state-employed authors are sometimes too biased. After all, people who actually work as state-employed authors are probably in a better position to comment about their own situation. I think that many state-employed authors share the same mutual feeling on the topic of politics and literature:

"If I write books purely for the purpose of expressing my thoughts and feelings, then I should have a say in the things that I write. Therefore, please don't tell me what to do. Living as an author in this country is already not an easy task. Please do not add to our troubles."

My friends all have a fixed stipend as a state-employed author and when I see their stable and tranquil lifestyle, yet hear about their doubts concerning their current occupation, I find myself hesitating to include them in the book. In the end, it is probably better to leave them out in order not to disturb their current livelihoods. If I name my friends in this book, it is quite possible that they will be invited for tea with their superiors. Thus, I have decided to leave them out of the book, and let them quietly enjoy their lives.

We are friends after all, and friends support each other. What right do I have then to intrude upon their peace?

_ END OF BOOK _

www.ingramcontent.com/pod-product-compliance
Lightning Source LLC
Chambersburg PA
CBHW060511280326
41933CB00014B/2929